Remarking on Releford

"From where I sit, Travis made himself into the glue of this team. He stuck to it, he persevered, and through sheer hard work became an invaluable teammate. As a former coach, I know that the attributes Travis brought to the court are the kind that make teams better. We saw that first-hand at Kansas."
— Sheahon Zenger, Athletics Director,
University of Kansas

"As long as I've been a college head coach, I've always had a great deal of respect and admiration for players who get better each and every year. That's exactly what I saw Travis Releford do from a distance. From my perspective, Travis clearly understood his role and his value to his team, and he exemplified what a true team player should be. He was a very underrated player during his career at Kansas. And when you look at what he gave to his team in terms of winning plays, I'm not so sure that he may not have been the most valuable player on that Kansas team during his senior year. The final thing that stood out to me about Travis was how he appeared to truly enjoy his time at Kansas. You say to yourself, now there's a guy who truly embraced his college experience and got the most out of it."
— Rick Barnes, men's basketball coach, University of Texas

"Travis was the 'heart' of the Kansas team. He did so many positive things for them in every phase of the game. He could score, but his defensive play and leadership may have been even more important. He is a really nice young man who cared deeply about his team."
— Roy Williams, men's basketball coach,
University of North Carolina

"When I think of Travis Releford, I think of someone who's a winner, who's tough and is a hard worker. In addition to all of that, though, Travis is extremely polite, and is fun to be around."
— Bonnie Henrickson, women's basketball coach,
University of Kansas

"Travis is one of the most confident guys I know. Some of the best memories of him are from pick-up games and he'd miss a couple shots in a row, and then somebody will give him a hard time. Big mistake. He'll say, 'Alright, guys, I'm turning the switch on.' Next thing you know he doesn't miss at all."

— Kevin Young, former Jayhawk

"Trav is a brother to me. As far as roommates, he was great. He never got on my nerves and I don't think I ever got on his nerves, although I probably wouldn't have known if I had because he was so cool with everything. Off the court, everybody liked Travis. And since he was from Kansas City, people had known about him for years. When we weren't in season, we'd go out to a club on the weekend or whenever and everyone knew who he was and they loved being around him. I learned so much from him and have so much respect for him. Like I said, he's my brother."

— Tyshawn Taylor, former Jayhawk

"Bill (Self) was kind enough to let me hang around when I wasn't working, so I saw a lot of the practices and games when Travis was playing. You can't value what he does, statistics-wise; you just value the impact he has on the game. He does all the little things that you don't necessarily teach — he guards the best player, he gets every loose ball, every long rebound, you know he'll get all those 50-50 balls, he makes simple plays, and he makes his teammates better. When you look at the box score, it doesn't always tell the story and the contribution he makes. I'm just a big fan of what he did, how he conducted himself, and all the things he did to make KU better."

— Larry Brown, Hall of Fame coach,
Southern Methodist University

"Travis is a young man who was at Kansas for five years but enjoyed the process of college athletics. He came in, played, took a redshirt, and then continued to play and get better. There were grumblings early in his career, but he ended up starting in a national championship

game and became a team leader. He put himself in a position where he'll do very well in life. I'm so happy for him and proud of him. I've followed him for a long time. These are the stories that need to be told about college athletics. This is a great story and the way a lot of college stories should play out."

— Danny Manning, former KU assistant coach and current head coach at Tulsa

"Travis gets 'it.' I don't know that he got it when he first got here — very few people do, but it didn't take him long to get it. It didn't take him long to understand that we all benefit if we win. It didn't take him long to figure out that there are other good players here and I might have to work my butt off for awhile and wait for my time. He's matured since he's been here. From a standpoint of reading people and understanding people, he's mature way beyond his years. He wants to have fun but he's businesslike. He's pretty much a coach's dream to coach. He may not be great at a lot of things, but he's good at everything. He believes he's great, though, which is one thing I love about him. He's competitive. Coaches a lot of times get credit for a guy's development. Trav's development falls on his shoulders because his attitude and his will are what make him good and what got him better."

— Bill Self, men's basketball coach, University of Kansas

RELENTLESS

FROM REDSHIRT TO THE ROCK OF THE JAYHAWKS

TRAVIS RELEFORD

WITH MATT FULKS

FOREWORD BY BILL SELF

Requests for permission should be addressed Ascend Books, LLC, Attn: Rights and
Permissions Department, 12710 Pflumm Rd., Suite 200, Olathe, KS 66062.
10 9 8 7 6 5 4 3 2 1

Printed in the United States of America
ISBN- 978-0-9893095-1-6
ISBN: e-book 978-0-9893095-2-3

Library of Congress Cataloging-in-Publications Data Available Upon Request

Publisher: Bob Snodgrass
Publishing Coordinator: Beth Brown
Editor: Jim Bradford
Dust Jacket and Book Design: Rob Peters
Sales and Marketing: Lenny Cohen, Dylan Tucker

All photos courtesy of Travis Releford unless otherwise indicated.
Front cover photo courtesy of AP Images.

This book is not an official publication of, nor is it endorsed by, the University of Kansas.

Every reasonable attempt has been made to determine the ownership of copyright. Please
notify the publisher of any erroneous credits or omissions, and corrections will be made
to subsequent editions/future printings. The goal of the entire staff of Ascend Books is to
publish quality works. With that in mind, we are proud to offer this book to our readers.
Please note, however, that the story, the experiences and the words are those of the author
alone.

Printed in the United States of America

www.ascendbooks.com

Table of Contents

Dedication

To all of the KU fans, who make being a Jayhawk an incredible experience. I'll never forget the love you guys showed. Rock Chalk, Jayhawk!

Acknowledgments

First off, as I mentioned in my senior speech, I want to thank God, who makes all things possible. I want to thank Coach Self. If it weren't for him, Tim Jankovich, Danny Manning and the other coaches at KU, I wouldn't be writing this book today. I'm biased, but I don't think there's a better program in the country than KU and definitely not a better coach or person than Coach Self. Thank you to Coach Zych, who allowed me to transfer to Bishop Miege and then was a great influence. To L.J., who is a great influence, mentor, coach and friend. To all of the fans, who add to the excitement and fun of playing basketball. To all of my teammates, who are brothers for life. A special thanks to Ty and Mike, who have always been there for me. Thanks to Matt for helping me write this book. Special thanks to my family (if I don't name you personally, I'll apologize now), who have been supportive throughout my entire life: Deandre, Tracy, Trevor, Tamara, June and Katelin. To my dad and mom, Tracy and Venita: I love you. Finally to Jenn and T.J., who give me another reason to keep working hard and keep chasing my dream of playing professional basketball.

As one might imagine, compiling a book such as this is quite a task. The following people were instrumental in the authors being able to put this book together:

To Bob Snodgrass, Beth Brown, Jim Bradford, Rob Peters, Dylan Tucker, Lenny Cohen and the rest of the team at Ascend Books for giving the opportunity to tell this story and then for the guidance to turn it into an incredible book.

To Justin Zanik and J.R. Hensley at ASM Sports. Besides working hard to make sure I ended up in the best professional playing situation, Justin was a key in helping this book get off the ground.

To Darin Snapp, who bleeds black and gold but stepped up with some invaluable research.

To Coach Bill Self for agreeing to write the Foreword, not to mention letting the authors harass you for more quotes throughout the book. Special thanks to Jim Marchiony, Associate AD at KU, and Chris Theisen, KU's Assistant AD for Communications, each of whom was a great influence early in this project and then a tremendous resource and asset throughout the writing.

To each person who agreed to be interviewed and to those who provided quotes. Thank you for your time and your willingness to be part of this project. It's an honor to have each of you in here.

And, from Matt: Thanks to Travis for agreeing to let me help tell your story. To Chris Browne, who's a great friend and sounding board (even if he is a Tiger). To my interns with the Kansas City T-Bones, Emily Park and Danny Jones, as well as the rest of the front-office team, who helped during the writing of this. To the friends and family who always serve as core encouragement and guidance, a world of gratitude is owed: Jim Wissel, Tom Lawrence, Chris Garrett, the Treeces, the Brownes, Josh and Susan. As with past book projects, based on the amount of praying I did during the writing of this, without Christ this isn't possible. A final special thanks to my favorite

ACKNOWLEDGMENTS

in-laws, Todd and Pat Burwell, and my parents, Fred and Sharon. To Helen, Charlie and Aaron, who make me thankful each day; and, to my best friend, Libby, who loves me in spite of my quirkiness and shows me that it takes a special person to live with an author on deadline.

Thank you, all.

Foreword

Many times, toward the end of the 2012-13 season, I referred to Travis Releford as "The Rock" of our basketball team. His leadership from the time he arrived on campus — through boot camps, practices, games and how he handled himself in the classroom — was a prime example of how any college coach, regardless of the sport, would want all our student-athletes to act.

Travis was a winner first. Players like him are how we win championships. He was a part of five Big 12 regular-season titles, three Big 12 Tournament championships, four Sweet 16s, two Elite Eights and one Final Four, where we were so close to winning the title. When Travis was at Kansas he did not care about individual points, accolades or anything like that. I said during his sophomore year he'd be a 1,000-point scorer while at KU. He ended up 35 points short but that didn't matter because all he wanted to do was win and he worked at that every day he was here.

Travis was a young man we recruited longer than anyone else. Ever since we came to Kansas in 2003, Travis was a target. We felt like we knew Travis and his family very well. We watched him play so much and watched his development over time in high school and AAU ball. When we got him here we thought he would be a great defender and eventually be a terrific player. And we were right on.

Travis had an up and down career his first three seasons. He averaged just seven minutes a game his freshman year, yet clearly showed that he was going to be solid on the defensive end. Then he took a redshirt season when we knew he really didn't want to. We knew it was best for his life and he followed our lead and it eventually paid off.

His sophomore year he hurt his ankle at Michigan, missed six games and struggled to crack the rotation the rest of the season. Prior to the injury he was in our rotation and scoring just over six points per game.

As a junior "The Rock" took off. He became a team leader on and off the court. No one in practice or in games wanted to go head-to-head with Travis. His hard work during the offseason paid off; he moved into the starting lineup and stayed there. His durability those final two seasons was phenomenal. He averaged 31 minutes per game his junior year and 34 as a senior. Jeff Withey was the best interior defender in the nation — he was named the co-NABC Defensive Player of the Year — but there's no question Travis was the best perimeter defender in our league. I'm not the only coach who thought that highly of him. The conference coaches named him to the All-Big 12 Defensive team and I wasn't allowed to vote for him. The league's coaches also named him All-Big 12 Second Team, and he and Jeff were locks for our Danny Manning "Mr. Jayhawk" Award.

In his new book "Relentless," Travis takes readers on a journey throughout his life, which hasn't been perfect, and shows us the highs and lows, and the type of determination needed to be a successful college athlete. And he was that.

Travis was truly our Rock. Throughout his career at Kansas he showed grit, toughness and perseverance. In short, he showed what it takes to be a winner and the rest of the guys fed off of that. I don't know that there's been anyone here who

FOREWORD

I've had more confidence to put on another team's best scorer. There hasn't been anybody here who I've enjoyed coaching more than Travis.

He earned his degree from KU in four-and-a-half years. He's going to be an unbelievable father and an unbelievable husband because he's an unbelievable person.

— Bill Self

Introduction

Stories have a funny way of finding writers.

During the 2012-13 basketball season, I started to think it was time to collaborate on another KU-related book. Specifically, there were at least a couple of players who seemed to be good stories. So, I emailed two of my contacts at KU to get their opinions. The answer from each was nearly identical: "(Player X) is a great kid and would be an interesting story, but I'd definitely go with Travis Releford."

Of course, as happens, life got in the way and I never contacted Releford (or "Player X"). By June, knowing he was getting ready for the NBA Draft and then whatever was next in his professional career, and with summer being my busy time of the year, I figured there was no reason even to think about a project with Releford.

But stories have a funny way of finding writers.

During the last week of June, I ran into publisher Bob Snodgrass of Ascend Books, who said he was meeting with Travis Releford about a book, and asked if I'd be interested in working as Travis's co-author.

After a series of meetings and quick research, I decided that I could take on the project, in addition to another book and my work as the Director of Media Relations for Kansas City's minor-league baseball team, the T-Bones. (Sure, I wanted a challenge!)

And, admittedly, there were times during the writing of this book, when things got especially chaotic, that I questioned my sanity. I wondered why I was working on this book.

But then it hit me; almost a "Field of Dreams" moment. Working on "Relentless" was changing me. It was an eye-opening experience that nailed home three facts: life isn't fair; reality is oftentimes different from perception; and nice guys might finish first, but they have to work incredibly hard to get there.

See, the perception of Travis Releford is that, playing for a top AAU team and being a product of Bishop Miege High School and then the University of Kansas, life's been easy. Things have been handed to him on a silver-covered basketball rim.

The reality is that Travis Releford has been through more and has seen more than most of us who'll read this book. Growing up in a rough neighborhood of Kansas City, Mo., oftentimes not knowing whether there'd be food on the table, and starting his high school career at Central High School, Travis *chose* to change high schools in an attempt to improve his chances of playing basketball. That decision turned into him getting a solid education at one of the top universities in America, and helped prepare him for a professional basketball career. He's become proof that dreams can come true.

There have been countless times during his life that Travis Releford could've given up: on those around him, on himself, on life. But he didn't. In fact, whenever he's been faced with adversity, Travis has worked harder and tried to rise above the commotion. More often than not, his determination and hard work have won out. He's been "Relentless."

We've all been told how it's important to learn something new every day, regardless of your age. This project has been a wonderful learning experience for me. I'm a better man for getting to know Travis Releford and working on this book with him. Our hope is that you can say the same thing after reading it.

— *Matt Fulks*
August 2013

2011-12: A Dream Nearly Realized

Any kid who's an athlete, whether he's in organized sports or not and regardless of the sport, imagines himself in the "big game." He sees it on TV or hears about it and wants to be there, to experience it, to be involved in the final play for "his" team.

For me, growing up in Kansas City, that meant the Kansas Jayhawks.

I committed to Kansas in June 2007, the summer before my senior year at Bishop Miege. As every KU fan remembers, that next season was a magical one for the Jayhawks, as they beat Memphis in the national championship game in San Antonio. Watching that tournament cemented that I'd made the right choice in picking Kansas.

It also made me believe that I might be able to experience that — to live my childhood dream — as a player one day.

Fast forward four years, to my junior year at KU. (I was a redshirt after my freshman year, which you can read about later in the book.)

After losing the twins, Marcus and Markieff Morris, Tyrel Reed and Brady Morningstar — four starters and four of our five leading scorers from the previous season — 2011-12 was supposed to be our down year. We heard that throughout the season and then as the NCAA Tournament got closer. It was a great feeling to get ready for the tournament with a 27-6 record because we kept going out and proving each game that we had good experience and guys who stepped up and performed ... even though it was our "down year."

On Selection Sunday, the day they announce the tournament brackets, we have dinner as a team and then, once the brackets are announced, we talk about our region and who's on our side. Then, like any other fan, we debate which teams got the easier brackets.

Throughout my career, there were times we didn't get a good bracket and other years where it was drawn up for us to go all the way. Either way, you can't look too far ahead. Coach Bill Self stresses that each weekend is a two-game tournament. We weren't going out to win six games in a weekend.

After back-to-back seasons of disappointing NCAA Tournament losses to Northern Iowa and VCU, we found out on Selection Sunday 2012 that we were the No. 2 seed in the Midwest Region. On paper, it seemed like a tough schedule. North Carolina was the No. 1 seed in the Midwest, with Georgetown as the 3 and Michigan as the 4. Not an easy road to the Final Four.

There wasn't as much pressure in the 2012 tournament as a second-seeded team, definitely not as much as we'd had the previous to years as a No. 1 seed. When you're a No. 1 seed, besides feeling that you have to live up to that seed, you know, also, that you're getting every team's best shot. After all, the whole world is against you, or at least that's how it feels, because fans always want to see the favorites lose.

As a No. 2 seed, the opposite could be said. Because we weren't a top seed, we felt we had a lot to prove.

Opening Game: Detroit

Our first game was against Detroit in Omaha, Neb., which is only a few hours from Lawrence. KU fans travel great, regardless of where we play, but we knew there'd be a lot of

Jayhawk blue in the arena. With the way the NCAA Tournament pod system works, Missouri, as a No. 2 seed in another region, was in Omaha, too.

We weren't going to overlook Detroit. Even though we had trouble with the teams that we didn't hear much about, like Detroit, we're all too familiar that every team has at least one guy who could get 20-plus points on any given night. Plus, if they're in the tournament, they're capable of beating any team.

Our past history of losing to teams like Northern Iowa and even Bucknell and Bradley years before us, prepared us to be ready for Detroit. Being a high seed doesn't give you a shield from upsets.

Proving that point — and possibly helping us focus more — by the time we hit the court against Detroit, two other No. 2 seeds had lost — Duke and Missouri. We didn't want to be the talk of the town as another second seed to lose, especially with the Tigers falling already. Watching those games pumped extra energy into us.

So, it shouldn't be too much of a shock that we came out loose against Detroit. They were close in the early minutes, even leading by two points in the first three minutes, but we never really struggled.

The biggest struggle might've been for my roommate, Tyshawn Taylor. He wasn't struggling with Detroit; he kept fighting muscle cramps. I remember looking down the bench one time when he wasn't in the game and realized that he'd just disappeared. We found out later that he was in the locker room getting fluids through an IV. Ty couldn't do anything about it, but we definitely made sure we gave him a hard time about leaving us hanging out there.

Elijah Johnson ran the point in Ty's absence, and did a great job. He ended up as our team's second-leading scorer with 15 points, one behind Thomas Robinson, including a game-high three 3-pointers.

We ended up cruising to a 65-50 win, which set up a second-round game against Purdue.

Round of 32: Purdue

Although Purdue was a No. 10 seed that beat seventh-seeded St. Mary's in their first game, we knew they gave us a match-up problem with Robbie Hummel, a 6-foot-8 shooter who played the four spot.

T-Rob didn't get to play against guys like that and we couldn't put Jeff Withey on him. So, we knew they had a match-up advantage, but nobody could have predicted the type of disadvantage we'd be facing.

Hummel started the game shooting lights out. It didn't matter who was guarding or where on the court we got him, Hummel couldn't miss. He hit his first four shots, including three 3-pointers. Adding to that, Tyshawn, Kevin Young and I all picked up two early fouls and had to sit on the bench during the first half. Not to mention, we came out with horrible shooting. We made only two of our first 17 shots in the game and missed all seven of our 3-point attempts. Midway through the first half, Purdue went up by 11 points.

By the end of the first half, Hummel had 22 points and Purdue led 36-30.

In the locker room at halftime there wasn't a sense of panic or guys being in a bad mood. We just kept saying that there was no way Hummel could keep shooting like that. As Coach Self went over the stats and the breakdown of the guys, everything seemed OK. He echoed our thoughts, of course, that Hummel couldn't come out shooting the same way in the second half. The key was figuring out a way to make that happen. We couldn't let him get shots and then hope that he missed — he had proved in the first half that he wasn't going to miss.

Much like we planned, we used a box-and-one defense in the second half, with me guarding him, and it threw him off. That's when the game changed.

Throughout my career at KU, I became known as a tough defensive player. I take a lot of pride in my defense because it can help our team win. If that's what my role is supposed to be, that's what I'll do. All through AAU ball and high school, I always wanted to be the guy to guard the toughest player. I have no idea why I've had that mentality; it just happened. But, it was always a way to help our team out.

As was so often the case for our Jayhawk teams, defensive play keyed our offense.

Late in the game, as we'd battled back, two plays stand out to me. With less than 30 seconds left and Purdue up by one, Elijah grabbed a loose ball and went down and hit a shot, giving us a one-point lead.

Then, Hummel missed a 3-pointer, and Elijah threw a lob to Ty for a dunk. They had one last attempt at a 3-pointer that would've tied the game, but they missed.

We survived, 63-60, and earned a trip to the Sweet 16 in St. Louis against North Carolina State.

> *"Even though, because of the redshirt, Trav was a year behind me, he was as much of a leader on the team as I was. T-Rob and I were the type of leaders who'd yell, but Travis was always the cool-headed one who'd pull everyone together. I remember a specific moment against Purdue, when we were trailing —as we did that whole game, I think — and Travis pulled everyone together and said, 'Guys, we've been here before. We've been down to Missouri by 19. We've been down to Duke and came back. We've been down big and come back. We just need to stick with it.' He did that right before Elijah hit a big shot that gave us the lead with less than a minute. Trav's always been the calm, cool and collected leader. I've always been the one yelling, trying to get guys going, but Trav is the one to calmly say, 'Relax, we got this; we've been here before.' That's what he kept telling us against Purdue."*
>
> *— Tyshawn Taylor*

Sweet 16: North Carolina State

N.C. State was an 11 seed, but we couldn't overlook them at all. Watching film, it was obvious they had a really talented team. They had guys who could shoot. They had two legit big men in CJ Leslie and Scott Wood, who were scoring threats and could give any team problems. Plus, we knew they'd be a challenge because they were experienced and well coached.

All of that could've spelled trouble for us. Unlike Purdue, they didn't have only one guy who could beat you or one guy we could overlook.

As we got into the game, that became even more apparent. They played to their advantages. About midway through the first half, they took a 10-point lead. They weren't shooting that well during the first half, about 34 percent, but they'd hit four 3-pointers. To make matters worse, we were only shooting 34 percent, and we'd missed all eight of our 3-point attempts.

With the Wolfpack leading 33-32 at the break, since we'd been down this road so many times before, we didn't panic. Neither did Coach Self or the rest of the staff. Just like he always does, Coach Self pulled out the stat sheet, broke down the first half and looked at keys to go ahead in the second half.

The second half wasn't much cleaner for us, but we picked up our defensive intensity and guys like T-Rob, Elijah and Withey stepped up big time. This game was a great example of the type of team we had that season. Tyshawn had a bad game offensively, scoring only six points on two-for-14 shooting, and missing all six of his 3-point shots, but T-Rob and Elijah picked things up. Robinson had a double-double with 18 points and 15 rebounds, and Elijah hit our team's only 3-pointer and scored 11 points. With those guys picking things offensively, Ty still ended the game with 10 rebounds (all defensive) and led the team in assists (five) and steals (three). And Withey? All he did was tie a KU record with 10 blocked shots. As we were in the middle of seeing, and continued to see in 2012-13, Jeff was a shot blocking king!

We ended up beating North Carolina State, 60-57, and earned a date two days later with one of their main rivals, North Carolina.

Probably my biggest memory of that game isn't the game itself but the seconds immediately after. As we were going through the line to shake their hands, they were telling us that they were pulling for us against North Carolina. I heard several times, "You guys gotta get North Carolina for us." You might've thought they'd be pulling for their in-state school, a team from their conference, but nope. They wanted us to beat the Tar Heels. I couldn't agree more!

Elite Eight: North Carolina

I don't know what it is but Coach Self has Coach Roy Williams figured out. Obviously they're both great coaches with great players but Coach Self seems to have Coach Williams' number. As a player for Coach Self, that couldn't help but give us some confidence going into the quarterfinals against North Carolina.

That was the most fun game we played up to that point. Since it was in St. Louis, I remember all of our family, friends and fans coming out to support us. It was a game you'd expect from the top two seeds in the region — not to mention two schools with our backgrounds.

Both teams shared buckets throughout the entire first half. North Carolina went up by four points less than two minutes into the game, and that ended up being their largest lead of the night. Coach kept telling us that we had to get stops. We obviously weren't getting it done because we heard him tell us that countless times during the half. We were tied, 47-47, at halftime.

To give you an idea of how close it was, looking back at the stats, there were 13 lead changes and the game was tied 15 times. Besides that game, there were only three other games during our entire season when we had double-digit lead changes and ties: one against Duke and both games against Missouri.

At halftime, guess what? No one panicked. Our coaches had

done a great job of scouting North Carolina. The Tar Heels had been doing what the coaches told us they'd do; we just weren't executing the scouting report.

We figured that we were lucky in the first half in the sense that, even though they were a great outside shooting team, they had made only two of their seven 3-point attempts in the first half. That wasn't going to last if we didn't change our defense in the second half. We couldn't let them continue to stretch the floor and shoot uncontested threes. So, we went to a triangle-and-two or a box-and-one, which threw their offense off. They were confused. I don't think Coach Williams expected us to do that because all of the film they had seen of us had us playing man-to-man defense. You could tell they didn't know what to expect or what to do.

As a result, we went on a couple big runs in the second half, including scoring the first seven points of the half. Although the game was relatively close throughout the second half, our defense shut down the Tar Heels in the last few minutes. They didn't score from the field during the final 5:46. In that stretch, we went on a 12-0 run.

"We preached to each other during that whole NCAA Tournament run that we'd been behind and we could come back. The first thing that helped us that season was losing to Duke in Maui. That changed our whole attitude about the season and how we were playing. We knew we had to execute more. We then lost to Davidson, which was another wake-up game. We got to the conference and lost to Missouri after we were up big to them. They made great plays down the stretch that helped them win that game, but to us we felt we gave them the game. So we played from behind all year. We knew we were a good team but we needed to execute on certain mistakes. When we got into the tournament, we beat Detroit and then played from behind the whole time to Purdue. Then

we got N.C. State and played from behind again. But that North Carolina game was our best game all year. We played amazing. Travis did a great job of holding Harrison Barnes (to 13 points). T-Rob and I started yelling at Trav when Barnes scored a few points, but then we realized after the game that Travis held him (to only 13), which was a big reason we won."

— Tyshawn Taylor

With about 90 seconds left in the game and us leading by seven, Withey blocked an attempt by Stilman White in the lane. The ball went to Tyshawn, who tossed it to me on the break, and I went in for a two-handed dunk. I've had memorable dunks in my career, but that was one of the biggest because of all I had been through in my career up to that point. Not to mention, that bucket pretty much sealed the game for us, as we went up 76-67. That was our last field goal.

In typical coach fashion, Coach Joe Dooley didn't think the game was over at that point and he made sure I knew. He kept yelling, "Get back! This game isn't over!" I couldn't help but laugh and just say, "Oh, yeah, this thing is over!"

Then, with 20 seconds left and us leading 80-67, I got a rebound after a missed North Carolina shot. We were headed to the Final Four!

At that moment, we felt we worked harder than any team in the country to get to where we were. Coaches were happy for us and, of course, we were happy for us. That was such an emotional season for our team. As things happened on and off the court, we kept growing closer. In my five years at KU, that's probably the closest the team had been, which was a key to how far we went in the tournament. We all depended on each other. We were so close off the court that we had a good feeling for how to play together on the court. My brother, Trevor, would come up from Alabama and hang out with us. He was shocked about how well we got along and how close we were off the court. We were close in all five years I was there, but that 2011-12 team was the closest. We went from teammates and good friends to brothers. To this day — and likely forever — if one of us needs something, we make sure we're helping each other. That was the key that year.

So, to be stuck on the interstate between St. Louis and Lawrence for six hours after the game was perfectly fine with us. We were having a blast on the bus, not even thinking about the game anymore. Driving into Lawrence a little before 2 a.m., not much was happening on Massachusetts by that time. When we got to the Fieldhouse, though, all of that changed. There were thousands of people — mainly students — ready to erupt as we strutted into the Fieldhouse with the regional championship trophy, our Final Four hats and the pieces of nets we'd cut down in St. Louis.

Fans filled one whole side of the Fieldhouse, all the way to the top. The media was there. Coach and a few players said a few words, and then it was done. I had never experienced anything like that before. I can't imagine what it must've been like for the guys on the 2008 team.

Final Four Week

Coach Self always made sure we were prepared for games. The Final Four in New Orleans wouldn't be any different. Part of that preparation was Coach telling us to go to classes, which had just resumed after Spring Break. Even though we'd be in Lawrence for only two days that week, we *wanted* to go to class to get some loving from our fans. Believe me, nobody missed class.

Coach tried to tell us how fun the whole experience would be during the week.

"Not a lot of people get to go through life and say they played in a Final Four," he said. "Embrace it and enjoy it but understand that we have a goal to accomplish."

We left a day early so we'd be able to experience one night of freedom in New Orleans. We started off with dinner at a restaurant on Bourbon Street, and then we were free to walk around until curfew. Unfortunately, since we were a day early, the Final Four crowd really hadn't started showing up yet. We weren't complaining, though.

After that first night, it was a business trip. We were on lockdown with a curfew of 11:00 p.m., in our rooms.

For the rest of the week, we practiced at a few of the high schools around New Orleans and then at the University of New Orleans, which had new facilities because of the damage from Hurricane Katrina.

I was in New Orleans for a tournament with Adidas Nation during high school, so I'd seen Katrina's devastation. During that trip, they took us to where the levees broke and we saw the neighborhoods that had been wiped out. I'll always remember in front of where houses had been, there was a circle divided by an X. Numbers in those quarters of the circle showed how many people lived and died there, and how many kids and how many pets lived there. That's very vivid to me. We'd drive down a street and see only one or two houses in what was once a vibrant neighborhood.

For practice the week of the Final Four, we went at mid-season speed but not as long. We enjoyed the Final Four and being in New Orleans, but we had more to prove. Not only to us but also to everyone going against us. Our fans thought we were the best team on the planet, but we had to prove that to everyone else. We felt we might as well go in and win it all.

We had three or four days to prepare for our first opponent, Ohio State, which is about the same amount of time we'd have to get ready during the season.

To Coach Self and the assistants' credit, they tried to treat this like any other game. Coach Self was very consistent in how he coached, and that didn't change just because it was the national semifinals. He's very superstitious. We do things at the same time. We eat the same food for pregame. Before every game, home or away, regardless of the opponent, he writes the same game plan on the board with a few changes. He goes over it in the locker room and then repeats it before we hit the court. We eventually could repeat it. Of course, none of us were brave enough or stupid enough to repeat it out loud.

31

Ohio State was a great team that year with players such as Aaron Craft, William Buford and Deshaun Thomas. Their key player, though, was Jared Sullinger.

We played them early that season in December at Allen Fieldhouse. Going into the game, Sullinger was questionable with back spasms. He'd missed the game before us and we kept hearing that he was both "likely" and "unlikely" to play against us. At the time, the Buckeyes were undefeated and ranked No. 2 in the country. We were No. 13 after losing two games early in the year.

We prepared for the game — both games, really — as if they were going to have Sullinger in the lineup. Being at home in December, though, we felt we'd beat them regardless of Sullinger's status. When we found out the morning of the game that he wasn't playing, our confidence skyrocketed.

That showed on the court as we won 78-67.

Throughout the rest of the season, we kept hearing all sorts of excuses of why they lost to us. None of the "excuses" pointed out that we were better that day; they focused, of course, mainly on how Sullinger didn't play. So that, along with the fact the rankings didn't really change, upset us.

So, heading into the Final Four game, we wanted to prove to everybody that we could beat them with Sullinger. That motivation brought a lot of excitement and enthusiasm to our team in the days leading up to the Saturday night game in New Orleans.

Going out onto the court at the Superdome for shoot around was crazy. We couldn't see the seats at the top because it was so high. Each March, as more NCAA Tournament games are played in domes, fans hear about how it's tough for shooters because of the background. Personally, I think the background and the size of an arena is all mental. Most of us played outside growing up, with no background at all. The backdrop outside is much crazier. It's all mental in a big arena.

Of course, there are some butterflies and excitement when you're playing on that type of national stage, but once the ball's tipped, it's a game and you get into a flow of what you know. That season, we knew how to get behind early in a game, and the Ohio State match up was no different.

Neither team looked good early, but they jumped out and got a lead just like every team in the tournament that year. Down 7-2, Coach Self called a timeout four minutes into the game. And he went crazy; just chewed us out. He was just being a coach. We had to be the relaxing presence as players. We told him to calm down and that we'd pick it up.

A few minutes after the timeout, with a little less than 13 minutes left in the half, I hit my first shot of the game. It was a 3-pointer on a pass from Conner Teahan that made the score 12-9 in favor of Ohio State. After getting a couple rebounds earlier, that was my first shot of the game. There's such a rush when you hit your first 3-pointer or get a dunk in a big game. That feeling is only magnified when you're in the Final Four.

The Buckeyes stretched their lead during the final 10 minutes of the first half. We were down by 13 points five times in the first half, all within the last 6:30 of the half. But we didn't give up.

With less than 10 seconds left, T-Rob got a big rebound on a missed shot by Craft. He passed it to Tyshawn, who got it ahead to me. I hit a layup with less than a second left that cut the lead to under 10 at 34-25.

When we went into the half, we gave each other the same speech because all teams jumped ahead of us in the first half. We gave them confidence but we had to come out and let them know that we weren't going to roll over.

After going over the stat sheet from the first half, Coach Self told us, "This is the last 20 minutes. You can lay down and let them win it or you can take charge." We took charge.

We were a completely different team in the second half, but we didn't really change our scheme in the second half like we did against Purdue and North Carolina. Against Ohio State, it was more about picking up the intensity, especially on the defensive end.

Jeff Withey was a huge part of that — no pun intended. By the end of the night, Jeff had blocked seven shots, which was an NCAA Tournament record in the Final Four. It seemed like Jeff was setting some type of shot blocking record every time we took the court.

I'd like to think that I was part of that defensive surge in the second half, too. Coach played me 38 of the 40 minutes that night. Most of the time, I guarded William Buford or Deshaun Thomas. I was out there to get stops and keep everything together. Coach realized he'd get something good out of it eventually. I had a decent night, as our team's second-leading scorer (15 points), including 4-for-4 from the free throw line, and six rebounds.

Then there was Elijah, who went crazy that game. He got his first career double-double with 13 points and 10 rebounds.

We ended up beating the Buckeyes for a second time that season, 64-62.

As Coach said in his press conference after the game: "It was two different games. ... They dominated us the first half. We were playing in quicksand, it looked like. And the light came on.

The press conferences for the NCAA Tournament are different than the regular season. During the regular season there might be just one or two players join Coach Self. Here we are hanging out before our press conference during the Final Four. Seated from left to right: Jeff Withey, me, Thomas Robinson, Tyshawn Taylor, and Elijah Johnson

We were able to play through our bigs; we were able to get out and run, but the biggest thing is we got stops."

And, as a result, we were going to be playing for a national championship about 48 hours later.

Louisville and Kentucky played after us, so we didn't know our opponent yet. It really didn't matter to us. We had a healthy dose of confidence — not cockiness, but we felt it was us against the world. Instead of watching the Louisville-Kentucky game in person, we went back to the hotel, relaxed and watched the game from there.

The heavy favorite — and eventual winner — in that game was Kentucky. Throughout much of that season, everyone was picking them to win it all, which was understandable because they rolled through most of the year with great freshmen players.

We faced Kentucky early in the season at Madison Square Garden, and they beat us by 10, 75-65. That was our second game of the year. Even after that loss, we felt confident that if we saw them again in the NCAA Tournament, we'd beat them. Coach John Calipari is a great recruiter, but Coach Self is rarely going to be outcoached. So, with 48 hours and a scouting report, how could we not have confidence that we'd be able to get it done with Coach Self?

There might've been a few times during my career when he *might've* been outcoached, but those times were rare. (Want to know something? If Coach feels he's been outcoached, he would've pointed it out to us.) But he knew Coach Cal's tendencies.

Most of the talk about Kentucky centered on their big, Anthony Davis. He was a great shot blocker but he wasn't a scoring threat. Michael Kidd-Gilchrist wasn't a big threat. Doron Lamb, Darius Miller and Marquis Teague were bigger threats on offense. We also knew that Terrence Jones could step back and hit threes. It really wasn't a Goliath-type opponent when teams faced the Wildcats. We knew the type of team we had, which was a shot blocker, a great inside scorer, guys who could drive and a tough defense.

Even though the countdown to the national championship

game was less than 48 hours and getting shorter, we weren't incredibly anxious or saying, "Man, I wish Monday night would hurry up and get here already." There wasn't a rush for it because

I've always taken a lot of pride in my defense and, of course, that wasn't going to let up in the National Championship game against Kentucky. Although much of the nation felt we were way overmatched and that we'd just let Kentucky walk over us, we had a lot of fight in this game. It's one of those frustrating games because we were making a late run but ran out of time.

it was our last game. We knew we'd be able to relax after that. Coach was telling us to not want to rush through it. He wanted us to relax, turn off our cell phones and rest.

Some coaches have been known to take guys' phones or ban players from Twitter and Facebook. Coach Self wasn't like that. In the case of the Kentucky game, all he had to do was remind us of the importance of avoiding distractions and sacrificing for the team. Guys did a good job of not being up all night or staying on Twitter, Instagram, Facebook or whatever. We were committed as a team, as one group, to doing what needed to be done to win the championship.

It wasn't about individuals; it was a culmination of our season of sacrifice. Going into the season, nobody expected us to make it this far. Even Coach had doubts at times about the team. Beating Kentucky was a chance for us to put a cap on the season.

The National Championship

If you've been paying attention to the theme of this chapter, or at least the theme of each of our tournament games that year, this won't come as a shock: we had a slow start against Kentucky. The first few minutes were OK, but once both teams got into rhythm, Kentucky stretched out their first-half lead. A good way to gauge that might be leads that each team had in the first half. Our biggest lead of the game was 15 seconds into the game at 2-0, and then two minutes later when we were up 5-3. Kentucky's biggest lead was 18 points, 39-21, with less than three minutes left in the half.

By that time, I'm sure all of America had written us off. We weren't happy with our play, that's for sure. Personally, I wasn't as aggressive as I should've been. Early in the game I missed some baskets and maybe shot too far out, not looking for my shot. It wasn't anything Kentucky did because I missed layups and open looks.

Our conversation at halftime was pretty much a recording of every other halftime during the NCAA Tournament that year.

We'd been in this situation a million times before, so we still felt we were in the game.

In the second half, every Jayhawk on that floor gave their all. Unfortunately, that night, it didn't turn out for us. We lost 67-59. You could say we ran out of time. If a few plays had turned out differently, the game would've ended differently. We started a run late and we could tell their shirt collars were getting tight.

Tyshawn made a "traditional" three-point play that cut Kentucky's lead to 59-50 with 4:17 left. Then, I got a rebound on a miss by Miller, and was fouled. We weren't in the bonus yet, so we got the ball after a TV timeout, and T-Rob was fouled on a shot. He made both free throws, which cut it to seven, 59-52, with 3:52 left. Then, with about 90 seconds left, T-Rob made two more free throws, which made it a 62-57 game. That's as close as we'd get it. With a minute left, Tyshawn had an easy shot blocked, and then with about 10 seconds left, Elijah was called for traveling on a 3-pointer that went in. That's five points, which would've made it a one-possession game with time on the clock. At that point, it could've gone to either team. But that's how this game goes sometimes.

That night belonged to Kentucky.

> *"If we had a minute and a half more in that game, we would've won. Kentucky went on an early run and had us down early. We got it down late to a couple possessions, but we ran out of time. From one to five they had great players — probably the best team I played against in college — but we were in that game. Playing from behind hurt us against them. To play from behind is one thing but to do so against a good team like that was too much."*
>
> *— Tyshawn Taylor*

There was no shame, of course, losing to them that night, but to be blunt, the feeling sucked. I don't know that any of us had felt that low because of a basketball game. Once we got back home, however, and saw how far we'd come as individuals and as a team, it was an incredible feeling to say we played in a national championship game. There have been great teams, even a couple in my five years, that didn't come close to playing for a national championship. We weren't the best team that year, but we were playing our best when we needed to, that late in the season. We were role players and bench guys who stepped up. The only guys who believed in us were the players on the court and the guys coming off the bench. That's how we felt during that entire 2011-12 season. That's why we were so close. Nobody expected us to make it that far.

Finally, in my KU career, I was living the dream. It's every kid's dream to play for the big schools in a national championship. I was one of the lucky ones to live the dream.

Growing up in Kansas City and with Kansas so close and so good, it was every kid's dream to be a Jayhawk. That part of my dream, at least, came true.

2 Childhood

To say I spent my entire life wanting to play basketball at the University of Kansas is an overstatement. It's safe to say that most kids in my neighborhood in Kansas City, Mo., don't grow up with dreams of becoming Jayhawks.

I grew up in a corner house in a minority neighborhood around 33rd and Prospect. Growing up I didn't think it was a bad neighborhood because that's all I knew. When I started going to high school at Bishop Miege, though, people would say, "Dang, you live there?" They'd be surprised, not in a snobby way; it's just not seen as the best area of the city. For me, it was home.

Sometimes that "home" wasn't always the safest. I've seen someone right after getting shot. I didn't see the actual shooting, who did the shooting or know the guy who was shot, but I won't forget the experience. I was in elementary school and headed to a basketball game and I heard the shot. Right after, I saw a guy holding his stomach and screaming for help. No one stopped. It's the idea that if someone sees a shooting, no one wants to get involved. It was true that day.

Several years later I had a neighbor who was killed on his front porch in a drive-by shooting. He laid there for hours as the police investigated. I was in high school when that happened. I

41

didn't see the shooting but I saw the after-effect of him being laid out and the police tape and the family screaming. It's a horrible experience and once you see it, you can't forget it no matter how hard you try.

Even though those types of things happened in our neighborhood, there was really only one time I felt remotely unsafe at home. During the summer before my sophomore year of high school, Kansas City had an incredibly high shooting rate. Looking back at the stats, there were 127 murders in Kansas City that year (up from 91 the year before). A large number of those were within a 10-block radius of my house. It seemed that one to three people, on average, were getting shot every day. That happened all summer. That's the most I worried about where I grew up. We lost a guy who played on our football team in the eighth grade. He was shot. It was an extremely sad time. There were funerals every day. What was really unfortunate was that the average age was probably 17 to 23. It was a gang war, at least that's what they were saying on the news. I didn't know what was happening. I didn't feel we were safe anywhere that summer.

Usually, our neighborhood was full of families that were striving to make it. Most of the time, my family, for instance, was lucky to live paycheck to paycheck. There were six of us kids growing up, with my older brother Tracy, who's a little more than a year older than me, plus our brothers Trevor, who's two years younger than me, and June (seven years younger), and then sisters Tamara (five years younger) and Katelin (12 years younger). Then, my mom had her boyfriend there, and he brought three kids to the relationship, along with brothers and cousins and nephews. Starting around my third grade year and going through high school, there were nine to 10 kids at the house all the time. Yes, it was a full house.

My grandma, Virginia Flowers, lived two houses away. My uncle lived there. My family was close. Mom had a sister and a brother. Her sister stayed about 10 minutes away. Everyone would always come to my grandma's house for various family gatherings. She played a big role in my life, especially at a young age.

Grandpa, Walter Flowers, who passed away several years ago, had a lawn mowing service. As kids, we'd go and help out during the summer. He paid us a little. We'd go in the yard and pick up trash before he and my uncle mowed. Those are some fun memories. Even when we didn't go help in the yards, we'd wait for them to come back so we could help unload the lawn mowers and put tools away. It was fun for us at the time because we wanted to be able to help. As we got older, Mom would ask us to cut the grass and we didn't want to. She had to practically force us to cut the grass. But it was fun to be around Grandpa.

Out of all of my brothers and sisters — we're all tight but, whether because of the close age difference or because we all played sports — I'm closest to Tracy and Trevor. Of course, Trevor and I always got into fights about everything. I'll admit today that most of the time our fights started because I was picking on him. I used to mess with him all the time. I was always into something; messing with them or doing something

I was 4 years old, messing with some kitchen utensils. I have no idea what I was stirring up — probably trouble. I like to cook today, though.

to get into trouble. Trevor didn't have a chance; to this day he has no chance.

"I wouldn't take it that far. Back then he would start the fights and he'd win the majority of those. He was a lot bigger than me. That's not the case today; I think I could hold my own. Outside of those fights, though, everything I know about day-to-day life I learned from Tracy and Travis."

— Trevor Releford

As a kid, I was a problem child. Like I said, I was always into something, always into some kind of trouble, and there was no fooling Mom. We played basketball in the house. Trevor would dribble inside the house, while I was always jumping and trying to touch the ceiling. I remember one time we were doing that and the ball shattered a glass table Mom had in the kitchen. We tried to blame it on our sister, Tamara. We said she bounced the ball and broke the table. Mom didn't fall for that at all. No way! We got into some major trouble for that.

"They had this game in the house called crack ball, which I didn't understand. They'd be playing basketball, defending each other, and hitting the cracks on the wall with the ball. There wasn't a moment in the house when a ball wasn't being bounced or tossed around. I remember when they broke that table, but I though they tried to blame it on June. Either way, of course I told the kid they blamed that it was OK. I was dating a man whose son came up to me and said, "Mimi, we broke the table because we were playing crack ball in the house." I don't remember getting that mad. I think they had broken me by that time. Why holler at them? They weren't going to stop. I don't think they broke anything else after that. It's funny to think now that the games they were playing then in the house led to where they are now."

— Venita Vann, Travis' mom

Mom used to have plants in the house and we'd hit those and blame that on one of our sisters. Mom didn't fall for that, either. She somehow always knew. Mom would discipline but she probably thought it was pointless because I was always getting into trouble.

I was probably Mom's biggest headache in terms of getting into trouble, and it wasn't only around the house. In the first grade at E.C. Meservey, my teacher called my mom and told her to come up to school and see how I was acting. I was running around class and wasn't paying attention. As I was running around in my own little world, I ran into my mom. I remember like it was yesterday. Let's just say what started out as a great day of running around the classroom and outside turned out to be not so fun after Mom saw me. Not at all.

"His teacher called me one day and said he was outside and wouldn't come in from the playground.

These are most of my brothers and sisters, plus a cousin: (from left) Trevor, Tracy, cousin Arthur in the plaid, June, and then me and my sister, Tamara, in the back.

All of the other kids came in like they were supposed to, but Travis was still outside. I told her that was crazy, so she told me to come and see for myself. Sure enough, he was out there by himself, playing. I gave him a big whooping. No one ever called me again from school. He understood I meant business. He was always special and the teachers thought that. He was a lucky kid. In the fifth grade he had a chance to get into the money machine, which was one of these machines that had cash flying around. He won about $38 in that. He got into stuff as a kid, but he never gave me any problems, especially after that day I went to his school."

— Venita Vann

"He was a little energetic, a little hyper, maybe. And, sure, sometimes he was bad and would get in a little

Here I am with my brothers (from left) Trevor, June, and Tracy.

trouble. That changed one day when Mom went up to school and saw how he was acting. She gave him a whooping in front of the class. Kids were hiding under the tables — they probably started making good choices after that day because of my mom."

— *Tracy Releford*

Even though I stayed in trouble during most of my elementary years, teachers and administrators at the school saw something in me. They'd tell Mom that I was a special kind of kid. I stood out. I wasn't great at one thing, but I was good at a lot of things. Hmmm ... that sounds a lot like my basketball career. Because they liked me, I got away with a few things. One time when I was sent to the principal's office, I went to another teacher's room instead. She thought I was getting rewarded by getting sent to her room to hang out. She didn't know I was supposed to be in

And here are my sisters, Tamara and Katelin, after I taught them to play Call of Duty at my place on campus. It looks like they're getting the hang of it.

47

the principal's office until they called for me on the intercom. That's when everyone figured out I was in trouble.

I was an average student who did just enough to get by. I wasn't on the honor roll, which was fine because I wasn't studying hard. I enjoyed drawing, which I did all the way up until high school, and that became more of my focus because I felt school was a waste of time.

You could say I was the kid who wanted to be the center of attention. The class clown, if you will. I was always doing something that I shouldn't have been doing so people would

We had to sell a certain number of candy bars to get your name in a drawing to get in the Money Machine. I sold the minimum, one box, and my name was in there. Some kids were working hard to sell seven or eight boxes and get their name in their more times. My name was drawn. I came away with about $36. I was the happiest fifth grader in Kansas City that day.

notice me. I wasn't a bully but I wouldn't take anything from anyone. I got into some fights until high school because I had a short temper. As I got older, I talked back to my teachers. Frankly, I didn't listen to anyone but my mom.

That's one thing about my mom, Venita, she was a strong woman, raised six kids — most of the time on her own — and she always stood her ground. We saw her break down at times, but she always managed to figure things out and get back on her feet. She made sure we were taken care of. She worked two or three jobs while I was growing up just so she could pay bills and have enough left so we could have food and clothes. She did everything in her power to make sure we had everything we needed and, sometimes, everything we wanted.

For me, that "want" was Air Jordan basketball shoes. My brothers and sisters probably wanted video games, but it was Air Jordans for me. Mom told me she didn't have money for the shoes, but she somehow figured it out and she got them. Always.

I loved those shoes so much that, in high school, as soon as I heard a new pair of Jordans was coming out, I'd start bumming money from people, or doing extra work, until I had the exact amount. Then I'd wait in line at midnight to get the latest Air Jordans. Of course, I caught on early that they were re-issuing the same shoes every few years. But there are people who still waited in line.

In fact, all of those pairs of Air Jordans made my first day at KU especially memorable. The very first day I moved in, I pulled up to the Towers to unload my stuff and fellow freshmen, Tyshawn Taylor and Quintrell Thomas, were out front and offered to help. As we were taking bags to the room, one of them said, "Dang, all you have are shoes!" It's true. I had only a few outfits but all the shoes I liked. (Yep, I was a sneaker-head in high school. I still am, a little.) The majority of the shoes in those bags were Air Jordans, with a few Adidas mixed in since I played on their summer-league teams.

Thinking about it, I'm not sure what made Mom so strong. I'm not sure if her attitude and personality came from my grandmother,

Virginia Flowers, or it was just her. With my dad not around, Mom was everything to all of the kids in our house. To this day, she and I are extremely close. I'm fortunate to have her as my mom.

> *"I'd like to think that I'm a strong woman. One big reason is that I have God in my life. I tried my best to be a role model to my children. I was a community kid, as were mine. I didn't fall between the cracks. Sometimes I probably shielded my kids too much and probably made them stay inside too much, but I didn't want them to get hurt in the areas where we lived. The neighborhoods weren't that good. But I think we all did OK."*
>
> *— Venita Vann*

During the last several years, going back to high school, the story of my dad Tracy being in prison became common knowledge. It's been mentioned in newspaper articles and a local TV station even did a story on him.

He went to prison when I was just a few months old. Mom didn't try to hide the fact from us. She didn't tell us he died or ran out on us or anything like that. We knew he was in jail. We regularly went to the Western Missouri Correctional Center in Cameron, to visit him. We didn't know much about why he was in there or for how long. In fact, after every visit, we'd ask Mom, "When is Daddy coming home?"

"Soon," was the only answer she gave us. She never gave us a date or details; it was only "soon." We started to find out the truth in middle school. We were told what happened and why he was sentenced to life in prison.

> *"It was tough on me as their mother to take them to see their father. When we would go see him they'd want to search us to make sure we weren't smuggling drugs or weapons or whatever. The kids didn't understand that. We always had a good visit. They got to sit with him and talk. After the first couple years, though, it*

got to be too much and I never did it any more. They still talked to him on phone and wrote him letters. Then, when they were old enough, they could go see him. But the reason we didn't tell them why he was in there was because we wanted them to be older so they could understand. I think they knew all along that he hurt someone, but once they found out what happened, they never asked me about it again."

— Venita Vann

I don't know all of the details but, basically, Dad and a guy got into it one day. The guy threatened to kill my mom, my brother and me. The way Dad was living, he knew — or at least felt — the guy was serious, and he didn't want to sit back and wait for that to happen, so he took actions in his own hands.

You can think what you want but I've never thought Dad was a bad person. He did what he felt he needed to do to protect us.

Once I got old enough to get a cell phone, Dad and I started talking regularly. He does a great job of staying in touch and checking up on me to make sure I'm doing what I'm supposed to be doing. He's making sure that we're staying out of trouble.

Dad would say often, "If you're going to do something that you want to do; you have to give it your all. You're only going to get out what you put in." Growing up, he didn't know I was one of the top players in the city and going to Kansas until I went to Kansas. He'd get calls from reporters or people would send magazine articles to him. He'd then call me and jokingly tell me, "You know, I can still take you." (He's only about 5-foot-8. Mom's only about 5-foot-7. Tracy is about 5-foot-7. It's crazy that I ended up 6-foot-6.)

Another thing he stressed is that, "Trouble is easy to get into but hard to get out of."

"We may not have always had the best things in life, but Mom tried so hard to get us up to see Dad, so I was always appreciative whenever we went to see him. Our father is a lot like Travis in that he wouldn't let us see the down side of himself. He wouldn't talk

negatively. He was always positive. He'd always tell us that he'd be getting out "soon" — it was always "soon." Even from behind bars, though, he was trying to teach us and give us life lessons."

— *Tracy Releford*

Growing up there was a court right across the street, at Linwood Park, which is where we all started playing ball. We'd go over there every day. I don't think there was a day growing up in that neighborhood that we didn't go over there. It didn't matter if it was cold or wet or whatever, we'd be over there. There was dirt all around it, so when it rained, the court got pretty muddy, but it didn't matter. We'd still go over there. That was about all we could do. The only thing I wish is that it would've had lights, then we would've been able to play all night. At the time, we'd do 2-on-1 with Tracy, Trevor and me. We'd switch on and off who was the one. Looking back, we were just doing it for fun, not thinking about how much it was helping us.

> *"We played a lot of two on one, and also one on one, where the guy who got scored on had to leave the court. Travis and I would try to take the ball from Trevor — give him a little beat down — but today we'd have to ask if we can have the ball from him. I don't know if we could take it from him now. We played some rough games. Some days you'd want to stay outside and develop a jumper."*
>
> — *Tracy Releford*

> *"It seemed like it was always me and Tracy against Travis. Or if they wanted to pick on me it would be the two of them against me. Playing with those two helped my game out a lot. It made me fearless, especially going against Travis, who I thought was the best player in Kansas City when I was growing up."*
>
> — *Trevor Releford*

I started playing organized sports when I was about 8 years old. Mom worked at Della C. Lamb, which is a community center. They offered sports and Mom was around guys who knew she had boys, so they encouraged her to bring us down to play. My first and probably favorite sport was football. Tracy and I played in Pop Warner together because we were so close in age. Trevor was young and not heavy enough to play on the same team as us. We were all dominant players on our teams, though. Tracy was running back and I was the tight end and defensive end. Trevor did it all from quarterback to defensive back.

When football season ended (and we won the championship), basketball season started. My uncle, Walter Flowers, was my very first coach in organized basketball. He hadn't even played basketball. He grabbed a bunch of the guys from the football team, got jerseys for us and let us play. We played every Saturday.

Then, for most kids, it was time for baseball. I played baseball one year, in the eighth grade. My cousin wanted me to try out for the team. I made the team but I didn't really like playing. I got hit one time in the middle of the back and that was it for me. I wish I had started at an earlier age.

It's funny how things work out, though. If I had started playing baseball earlier in my life, would I have gone that route? God has a funny way of working sometimes. That was about the time I was getting better and noticed more as a basketball player.

I don't remember the details, but at one of our basketball games when my uncle was coaching, we came across a team that played travel ball. Their coach, "Coach Paul," as we ended up calling him later, thought Tracy and I had talent and he asked my uncle if he could take Tracy and me to play in tournaments. Since Uncle Walter didn't have playing or coaching experience, he was all for the idea. His simple advice to us: don't let your man score and just have fun. We switched teams and he stopped coaching.

With Coach Paul, we traveled around the Kansas City area, maybe an hour or two away at the most, which was out of town for Tracy and me. We even went to St. Louis once, which seemed like a completely different country to us.

Around that same time — in seventh grade — I threw down my first dunk. It was at a Boys & Girls Club. People would come to games after that because I was dunking. I was about 6-foot-2 then (I'm 6-foot-6 now). I've always had bounce. I still do I just don't show it that much. Even at KU, guys would give me a hard time, saying that I didn't have bounce, and I'd just have to show them.

"To this day, I think he's one of the best high school dunkers ever to come out of Kansas City. He helped put the Eastern Kansas League on the map. He could put a show on. I've always said that Bishop Miege was good for Travis, but even more importantly, he was very good for Miege. We got other players because of him."
— Rick Zych, Releford's coach at Bishop Miege

As much as I loved basketball, I didn't really have a favorite NBA team when I was growing up. I just liked watching certain guys such as Michael Jordan, Kobe Bryant and Allen Iverson. Those were the guys everyone talked about the most and seemed to be on TV the most.

My love of KU started when I was in middle school, at least consciously. It was ingrained in me earlier than that. My grandmother is a long-time nanny for the Ward family of Russell Stover Candies. They're big supporters of the school. I've known them since before I started playing sports. So I've been around Kansas and hearing about the tradition for a while. I didn't really know it, though, until I was older.

Middle school is around the time, as a kid, you're playing around the house or the court at the park, and you're announcing a game countdown as you describe the moment of the national championship game. That's when I became a Kansas fan.

3 An Unexpected Move

By the time I got to high school, I was seen as a pretty good player, mainly getting recognized through AAU tournaments.

AAU was an incredible experience for me in terms of competition and what it taught me about the game of basketball. After playing for the KC Magic, in the eighth grade L.J. Goolsby noticed me at a tournament and told me after a game that he thought I was good enough to play in college one day and maybe even the pros. I was stunned. Besides just being out there to have fun, can you imagine being told in the eighth grade that you could play professionally one day?

You could say that L.J. recruited me along with my best friend, Mike Gholston. L.J. talked to us about his program and sponsorships. At the time, Mike's dad, Michael Sr., was coaching our AAU team. He knew he couldn't take us as far on the AAU circuit as L.J. because L.J. had been involved for a long time. The next summer, five of us left the KC Magic and started playing on L.J.'s KC Pump-n-Run team.

"Athletically at the time he was special. Then, when you meet kids and engage with them, you see things. With Travis it was obvious that he wanted to be

successful. And, obviously, he didn't disappoint. A couple specific games stand out from when he played for us. He was playing up on our 16U team as a freshman. We were in Las Vegas for the big AAU tournament, and Travis had 29 points against the Michigan Hurricane. That was a coming out moment for him. I thought, 'Whoa, he's doing this!' He had a set back with a broken foot the next season but when he was playing for the 17U team, we were at a tournament in Dallas when he made an incredible play. He got a steal at half court and drove down the right side. BoBo Morgan, who was 6-feet-10 and went to UCLA, was running down the court, right behind Travis. Travis went up, from one side of the rim to the other and dunked on BoBo. It was an incredible play. I'm not sure Travis knew how athletic he was."

— *L.J. Goolsby*

In recent years AAU teams and players have gotten a bad reputation, I think. There are some coaches who are more interested in getting something out of it for themselves instead of the kids. That shouldn't cloud all of the coaches and AAU

This was our Magic team in my eighth-grade year. (From left) Marlon, Dominique, me, Beaumont, Jack, Mike G, Tyler in the back with the sideways cap, and Riley.

programs, though. It's only a small number of coaches who are like that.

L.J., for instance, is all about the kids and helping them accomplish their dreams and goals in life. I never got the impression that he didn't want the best for us or that he was trying to ride any of our coattails. He's very laid back, cool and down to earth. If you ask anyone who knows him, they'd say the same thing. Seeing, at a young age, the way he carries himself and takes care of business, was a great example for me. It's good to have people like that around you.

AAU is great for guys to come from all over the country and play in various tournaments against top competition. It's also a great way to build friendships. There are guys I played with and against since my freshman year in high school that are friends to this day. Plus, you might play in college with some of these guys. Tyrel Reed and Conner Teahan, two teammates at KU, were two of my teammates on Pump-n-Run.

Being part of a top AAU team helped me get noticed, even before high school. The summer before my freshman year at Central High School, I received a letter I'll never forget — my first recruiting letter. And it was from Kansas...well, at least a school in the state of Kansas. It was from Wichita State. Coincidentally, former KU guard Mark Turgeon, who was on the Jayhawks' 1986 Final Four team, was the coach at Wichita State at the time.

As much as I've thought about it and tried to put it into words for this book, the feeling of that first letter is indescribable. I was so happy that a college program was contacting me about possibly going to school there and playing on their team!

Suddenly, I got another letter. And another. I would try to tell you the first few schools who contacted me, but I reached a point fairly quickly where I was getting at least five or six recruiting letters a day. At first, I tried to save them but it became overwhelming when the five or six a day turned into a dozen each day. It was getting so much out of hand that I stopped opening most of the letters. By that point, I knew that I wanted to go to Kansas, and somewhere along the line they contacted me. Granted, I wanted to experience all of the recruiting process and hear what other coaches had to say, but I knew at that point that I was going to have an opportunity to play at one of the top programs in the country and I didn't need to open a letter from the smaller schools or even most Division I programs.

When people see my bio in the KU media guide or remember me from high school, they mainly remember my time at Bishop Miege, which is fine, but I actually started high school at Central.

Being a freshman at Central was fun and intimidating. The school was huge with a couple thousand students. We had to wear uniforms to school so the kids who couldn't afford clothes wouldn't stand out. Or at least that was the rationalization. You could wear whatever shoes you wanted, though, so you could tell from the shoes whether one kid's family had more or less money. Looking at the gymnasium you would've thought we all were rich. It was huge! We had four or five courts plus a running track, and an indoor swimming pool.

At first, the classroom setting was great. At least it seemed that way as a freshman because I felt half of the teachers didn't really care about our education. Either they'd be there and not doing a lot of teaching or they wouldn't show up and we'd have a substitute, who was clueless. You think you had it easy whenever you had a substitute? It likely paled in comparison to us. For the most part, we were just hanging out in class: groups of people talking together, or people talking or playing games on their cell phones, and even people smoking in the bathrooms. I remember looking around the classroom one day and thinking: this is really happening! Nobody listened to the subs at all. Nothing was getting done in class. All of the subs were run over at Central. I felt bad but there was nothing I could do about it. Besides, I was having a blast!

In addition to the normal times of teachers being absent, I remember times when the teachers as a whole group were on strike, but we still had to go to school. Instead of getting subs, the entire student body sat in the gym the whole day. It was almost like a daycare.

Unfortunately, much like our neighborhood, the school wasn't the safest place in Kansas City. Fights were a daily occurrence. To enter the school, we had to go through metal detectors. That didn't always do the trick, though. One day during lunch, someone was stabbed in the neck with a box cutter. The person survived but he was within an inch of having an artery sliced.

Between the fights and the teacher strikes, it got so bad that every Kansas City news station was sitting outside every

This was my freshman year at Central. Yes, I was sporting the Air Jordan earrings and a grill.

day because something was happening, or at least that's how it seemed. I told myself I had to get out of there. I wasn't scared, but it wasn't safe.

And, contrary to what anyone might think, it wasn't about basketball.

On the court, things were fine. Our team wasn't great, so I was getting a ton of playing time and making the most of it. We went to a tournament in a small town in Missouri, and we won only one game. Somehow, I still got MVP of the tournament. Never in my basketball career did I see that. Usually it's someone from the championship team or at least the runner up. Coach Mark Johnson called me and told me they gave it to me. To this day, I don't even know how I feel about accepting that trophy because of how we played as a team.

At the end of the season, I was selected as the Conference Player of the Year. By then, KU and the other Big 12 schools were coming in to watch me play. So, basketball at Central wasn't a problem. Not directly.

The problem was academically. College coaches started asking about my grades and school. To put it bluntly, my grades at that time wouldn't have gotten me into any college.

Early in my sophomore year, L.J., my AAU coach and seemingly the only authority figure who cared about my future, went over my academics with me. The path at Central was not good. I wasn't getting any help from the teachers or administrators. As students we didn't know that you needed a certain GPA to go to college, along with the ACT score. I didn't find that out until L.J. discussed it with me. The kids around me didn't really care about college. For most of the kids at Central, it was about having fun, getting out and starting adult life. But I wanted to further my career as a player and a person, and play basketball in college. With that in mind, I decided I needed to transfer.

"Sometimes when kids don't have resources, they don't know what they need to do to accomplish certain goals.

AN UNEXPECTED MOVE

Even though I think Travis is a special young man, I would help any kid who wanted that kind of guidance. Travis embraced it. We discussed his future and had some hard heart-to-heart conversations. The key was keeping him focused on academics when everyone was talking about how great he played. Travis learned that to reach his goals, he had to lock in on academics."

— L.J. Goolsby

The transfer rules were pretty simple: if I went to another school in Missouri, I'd have to sit out a year before participating in sports, whereas if I went to school in another state (of course, Kansas being the most logical), I'd have to sit out only a semester. Even though I was getting great competition playing AAU, I didn't want to sit out a year. My girlfriend at the time, along with some other friends, were at Bishop Miege. That made the decision relatively easy.

I told my mom that I wanted to leave, we talked about the process and she finally said, "If that's what you wanna do, I'm on your side." A few days later I was shadowing at Bishop Miege. There was an interview to go to school, during which time they broke down all the rules and asked if I was willing to work. They said they'd call me back in the next couple days. A day or two later, they called and said I could start the following week.

All the while, I'd been talking with Bishop Miege's basketball coach at the time, Rick Zych. Once I was started thinking about transferring and thought Miege might be a possibility, we talked several times and looked at my options. I think he was excited.

To this day, people think he recruited me to go there. To set the record straight, that wasn't the case. I wanted to go there and I approached him. But people think that he came to Central or to my house and recruited me. He wouldn't go down to my neighborhood. Are you kidding me? I don't think he's ever been to my house or even in my neighborhood.

"It was a running joke across town that I did a good job of recruiting him. That's all it was, though — a joke.

There was a situation at Central with some violence and he and his mom contacted me. The only reason he wanted to go to Miege as opposed to another school was that he had friends there. I had just seen him at the William Jewell Tournament, so I knew he could play. The biggest transition was going to be in the classroom. Moving to Miege might've been his best move, not because of athletics but because he got into a school that was going to challenge him academically."

— Rick Zych

For the most part, no one at Central knew I was thinking about transferring, including our coach, Mark Johnson. At least as far as I know. Shortly before Christmas break in my sophomore season, we were at the Cameron (Mo.) Tournament, and had just finished playing for third place. While we sat around the locker room, I got everybody's attention and broke the news to them: "I enjoyed playing with you guys and getting to know you, but this is my last time playing with you because I'm transferring next week." It was so quiet you could've heard sweat hit the floor. Finally, Coach Johnson, who obviously wasn't happy about it, said, "We wish you the best. Good luck."

That was the last time we talked.

Rumors started going around that I was leaving because in Kansas City, when guys are good and they go to an inner-city school, 90 percent of the time they transfer to another school because the competition isn't good enough. That's the perception anyway. During my time I didn't care about going to another school because of the competition. Shoot, in AAU ball during the summer I was playing against the best competition in the country and getting noticed by major college coaches. For me, it was 100 percent about the drama that was going on and bettering my chances of going to college. The big schools were coming to Central to watch me and figure out who I was, so it wasn't because of the competition. If the school was better and I could've gotten a better education there, I would've stayed there. Period.

AN UNEXPECTED MOVE

This was an opportunity to do something no one in my family had done. My brother, Tracy, went to college but he didn't finish. My aunt went to a small school. I could be the first one from my family to go to a major university, play and graduate. I wasn't going to go to college if I stayed at Central.

The decision was gut-wrenching. I was young and I'd be leaving all my friends, including Tracy. Leaving that and then going somewhere I didn't know people, except for a few who weren't even in my grade, was tough.

Essentially, I went from Central one day to Miege the next. That was a complete culture shock in every way: atmosphere, race, academics, teachers, students ... everything!

The first few days at Miege were crazy. People knew I was coming because of the hype of basketball. That might've helped people be more welcoming. Regardless, they were extremely friendly, helpful, and wanted to get to know me. If I'd been a regular kid and start when I did, it would've been really tough. I didn't know how to interact with white kids when I went to Miege. Sure, I played with them on the basketball court but that's different. You don't see black and white and socio-economic differences on the court. It was a culture shock. It took me awhile to get comfortable with other kids and the teachers, but by my junior year, things were fine.

Of course, the main reason I went there turned out to be the biggest shock and struggle of all, academics. We went to four different classes for an hour and a half each class, instead of going to seven classes in a day. That was different. At Central when the bell rang to start class, the halls were still jammed. At Miege, a minute or two before the bell rang, kids were in classes with their pencils out. If I had skipped classes there, it wouldn't have been a pleasant outcome.

"Travis worked hard and made it through it. The teachers were exceptionally wonderful. They made sure we had a computer that he could use and worked hard with him on his homework. We knew it was

going to be tough. When we met with school officials the first time, they told us that it was a private school where people paid money to avoid the foolishness. Travis did a great job of avoiding the foolishness. There was one teacher — a math teacher — who had no idea he played basketball. She was sitting at her desk, reading the paper, while he was her class. She saw his picture in the paper. She was shocked. That makes me feel good because it means he was humble and not making a big deal about basketball."

— Venita Vann

It definitely wasn't fun, going from doing whatever I wanted to do, to actually following rules and going to class on time. I had to catch on fast. I had gone two years without structure. Suddenly, I'm looking at three hours of homework each night. I would come home and have homework, while my brothers and sisters would be hanging out. That stunk. I had to do the work, though, because I wanted to go to school there. Sometimes I'd have to stay after school to get more work done or to get extra help. After a while I got used to it. My senior year wasn't a struggle at all.

"People at Central would ask me why he left and I'd just tell them it was to better himself. And he did. He did a great job when he went to Miege; I was really impressed. He got his reading up, his test scores up, and he graduated. He and Trevor. I was very impressed with that. He had to put in a lot of work, and we saw how hard he was working, to keep his grades up. As far as basketball, the teams we were playing on in the inner-city, kids were trying to play one-man ball, looking out for themselves. For both brothers, to get out of the inner-city and go to a school where they teach team ball was great. That's a lot like life, which is team ball. In the real world, it takes a team. I'm glad they got out of the inner-city and went and played ball. That was a good move on their part

and on my mom's part. I joke that I was the sacrifice brother. Staying at Central was a great lesson for me and for them. It might've helped Travis and Trevor work a little harder. When you see someone going through some things, like drinking and drugs and getting into some scuffles, you need to learn from them. There were plenty of days when I was dealing with these things, and I wasn't a positive example but they could learn from it."

— Tracy Releford

To go along with the recruiting rumors, people have wondered how our family paid for me to go school there and how I was able to get to school so far away every day. I've never asked Mom about the financial side of it. Many private schools have

This is my good friend, Jack, and I while in high school.

scholarships or some other aid available. I'm assuming that's how it went for us. As far as transportation, my grandmother worked near the school, two or three minutes away, so she dropped me off every morning and then I could get a ride home in the afternoon. It worked out perfectly.

On the court, Miege had an excellent program. The year before I got there, they lost to Highland Park in the state championship. The big players at the time were Dominique Johnson and Isaac Miles, who was a senior during my first semester there. I wish I could've played with Isaac for at least a year because I think we might've won the state championship if we'd played together.

I was allowed to practice with the team but I couldn't start playing games until my junior year. In my very first practice, I got a chance to show what I could do. We had a 2-on-1 break with Jack Shortell as the player on defense. I had the ball in the lane and he tried to block me, but I dunked over him. The team hadn't seen me dunk before then. I didn't know Jack until after that dunk, but we became good friends. He's a class older than me and went on to play at Baker.

> *"When you look at Travis as a high school player, his dunks and deflections are the things I remember most. We had a couple plays that we'd bring out for him to dunk because that's what the fans, even on the road, wanted to see. Even though he had some great ones, his most memorable dunk to me remains that one against Jack. It was impressive!"*
> — *Rick Zych*

The toughest part of the transition to Miege was the school work. On the court, practices were more intense and we ran more drills, but it wasn't that tough system-wise. I caught on fast. To practice before my junior season made things easier because I could see what Coach Zych expected, along with his style and the team's style. It would've been tougher to catch on if I had been expected to play right away. Of course, Coach Zych remembers a conversation that I've completely forgotten.

AN UNEXPECTED MOVE

"After a few practices, Travis came to me and said, 'Wow, I can't do some of these things.' He wouldn't have started for us if he had been eligible immediately because he couldn't keep up with Isaac Miles at that point. He could score 30 points for Central, but we had more of a program. We weren't there to see how many points Travis Releford could score. I think that helped motivate Travis. He could go out and shoot and hit shots, but he knew his skills had to develop. His footwork wasn't great, and he had to work on his outside shot. He realized how tough it was going to be but his athleticism is off the wall, which helped him develop into a wonderful player."

— *Rick Zych*

We had a good team during my two seasons at Miege, but there aren't many specific games that stand out.

Our main rival was St. Thomas Aquinas, so every game against them was memorable because of the atmosphere and the fans. It was incredible to see all of the signs and students with their faces and bodies painted as they went absolutely crazy for their school. At Central, we'd have a few fans, but mainly family members. Miege, overall, was completely different, but then throw Aquinas into that mix and it was awesome. There was a full house every time we played them.

The highlight of my time at Bishop Miege was playing with my brother, Trevor. It's hard to put into words how blessed I was to play with him. Besides being a great brother, he's a great teammate and fun point guard. We played one year together at Lee A. Tolbert Middle School and, by that time, he was already dunking and becoming a great point guard. He was a great ball-handler, especially for his age. He made me look good with his passes and the way he played. He'd get the ball and throw it ahead to me on a fast break for a dunk.

Obviously, we had a great advantage, having played with our brother Tracy across the street from our house growing up. That helped us know each other's game better than anyone else. So I knew, for instance, that whenever Trevor had the ball, you'd better be ready to receive it. He could be looking in the stands and throw a perfect pass on the run. I knew when to expect it. Likewise, he's always known about my bounce. That knowledge helped both of us become better players. I could catch his passes and finish, which made him look good, which he is. And my stats looked better because of him throwing lobs and fast breaks. Coach Zych didn't play him much as a freshman. Once coach realized that guys would have to be ready, he played Trevor more.

The decision not to play Trevor as much as a freshman might've cost us the 5A state championship. In the semifinals, we lost to Highland Park, the eventual champion, 45-40. Our senior, who was a good scorer, had zeros across the stat line. At the end, we were either outcoached or outplayed. We ended up playing for third the next day and beat Kapaun Mount Carmel, 78-53. That was a year we were picked preseason to win the championship, and throughout the year it looked as if we would. If Trevor would've been in the game it would've been a different result.

Throughout that season, people started comparing me to some of the recent great players who came out of Kansas City: Anthony Peeler, Tyronn Lue and the Rush brothers. The talk didn't really add pressure, but suddenly I went from just a kid who played basketball because he loved it to someone who's ranked among the best in the city and throughout the country. I was happy to see that, but it was crazy how fast everything happened. I didn't really have time to feel any pressure. The key was to keep working and not let it get to my head. All of my coaches stressed that to me. It was the old adage of how sometimes it's easier to get to the top than it is to stay there.

By this time, coaches from North Carolina, UNLV, Tennessee, most of the Big 12 schools, including Kansas, were coming to our games. At first, it was overwhelming because it seemed there was a new school every day. Coach Zych hadn't experienced anything like that at the time, so he didn't really know what to do. Miege had really good players throughout the years, but they never had coaches like Bill Self, Roy Williams and Rick Barnes come in to watch a pick-up game or a practice.

"I thought it was cool to see the big-time coaches come in and watch him, especially when they'd be there for a pick-up game. Seeing the coaches there helped motivate me at the same time. Of course, it helped me to play with him and experience playing at a high level. That made me learn quicker and be more confident. If I messed up, I'd have to hear it from him. Every time. But that was good for me."

— Trevor Releford

It was funny. We'd play pick-up games and there'd be five or six coaches there. Coaches would walk around the school and visit my classes. Of course, all of them would wear polos with their school's logo, so you knew who was there. Since they'd seen me on the court — usually at AAU tournaments against some of the nation's top competition — and knew what I could and couldn't do, I guess they wanted to see our school environment and see how I interacted with other students and teachers. It was a chance to get to know me better as a person and see if I was someone they wanted in their program.

There was one time during my junior year when Roy Williams probably wondered if he wanted me in their program. Coach Zych wanted me to get more shots, so he made me play point guard the whole game. I wasn't turning the ball over but I was sucking and couldn't do anything right. North Carolina happened to be there that day. And we lost. That's the only time I played the point.

The basketball court wasn't the only place where I was getting a lot of attention. Because I could play a sport at a young age and had the attention of some of the nation's top schools recruiting me, I suddenly became the man of the house. In our community, to make it out you need to do so through sports most of the time.

You don't hear many people making it out as doctors or lawyers. Sports are a way of making it out. At a young age, I was getting a lot of attention from scouts, teams and schools. Because of that, my family looked up to me, I think. My family and coaches didn't experience anything like this.

I didn't wake up one day and say I was going to be the "man of the house." It just happened. The attention that colleges were giving me gave people in my family a reason to look up to me. It forced me to grow up fast so I could help them out. That remains true to this day.

> *"I think we all looked up to Travis, including Tracy. Sure, it was because of the attention he was getting, but during that process, he was growing up fast. He all of a sudden matured. We all saw him as the man of the house."*
> *— Trevor Releford*

Overall, I liked the recruiting process. At first it was exciting. Let's face it: it's cool to be in early high school and have schools contacting you. By my junior year, though, it was tiring. I was ready to end it. Believe me, it gets old when coaches are constantly calling or texting you. On top of that, recruiting services are calling to find out your top five or to see if you've made a decision. They all want to be first with the news, which is fine, but that gets old quickly.

In the spring of 2007, not wanting to waste anyone's time, I became the first in Coach Self's 2012 class to commit. I was tired of the recruiting process and didn't want to have to go through my last high school season stressing about it. I knew that's where I wanted to go, so why prolong it?

> *"Travis never wanted to go anywhere else other than KU. He loved Coach Self and Coach (Danny) Manning. The guy who put the icing on the cake was Coach (Tim) Jankovich, who was the first KU coach to come watch Travis. As the process went along,*

knowing he wanted to go to KU, if Travis had a big test, I'd call Coach Jankovich and he'd call Travis to encourage him to study. All of the big-name coaches came to Miege because Travis was an AAU legend — which is what I used to call him. All of them came through our building. Coach Self, though, and KU were the only coach and school he cared about."

— Rick Zych

The day after I made my decision official, the news media came and interviewed me. I didn't hold a big press conference

Ready for a rebound against Blue Valley West at their school. The Jaguars were a good team and a big rivalry, partly because they had Robert Lewandowski (not pictured), who was going to Texas Tech. So a guy at each school was going to a Big 12 school to play basketball.

with all of the different hats in front of me, representing the possible schools. That's one thing I've never understood because all you're doing is picking a school. It's a waste of everyone's time to hold a big press conference. For me personally, I don't like to sit through all of that stuff. For me, 30 seconds and it was over. That was more than plenty.

I was relieved it was over and excited about starting at Kansas a year later, but the person most excited with the news was probably my mom. She always wanted me to go to Kansas always because she didn't want me to leave. I was a mama's boy. She liked Coach Self and the coaching staff. When I called her — after I told the coaches I was coming — there's a good chance they heard her screaming all the way to Lawrence. We'll just say she was happy.

> *"He always said he wanted to go to KU, so I wasn't surprised but I didn't know he'd told the school he was coming. He called me and said he'd signed. I said, 'You're lying. I thought we were going to talk about it.' But he went ahead and did it. I was so excited. Besides*

This was during high school with two of my good friends, David Caton and Willie Reed. Willie went on to play for the Memphis Grizzlies.

going to KU, he was going to be going to college and getting a free education. I thank the people who were around him and were positive influences on him. He wanted to be around good kids, who act like they have sense and aren't out killing and robbing and stealing from people. He was around great influences with L.J. Goolsby, Kevin Jackson, and Michael Gholston — they're all great role models. They didn't forget about the kids. I thank those people. People didn't give up on Travis because they saw something special in him. I wasn't going to let him give up, but I'm so glad he didn't give up on himself."

— Venita Vann

Looking back at the recruiting process, I have only one regret: the official visit. I didn't take one. Not one. The official visit is a chance to visit the school on its dime and see the best of what it has to offer. The NCAA allows a certain number of visits for each recruit. Regardless of the sport or the school, athletic programs always want to put their best feet forward when recruits are visiting. I went to Oklahoma, but that was on Tyrel's visit. Coach Jeff Capel was the Sooners' coach and he's good friends with L.J., my AAU coach, so I was just there to hang out.

I didn't even officially visit Kansas! I went to Late Night in 2004, when Wayne Simien, Keith Langford and J.R. Giddens were there. (A funny side note is that I ran into Giddens in the summer of 2013 in Las Vegas when I was there playing for the Denver Nuggets' summer league team. I told him how much I looked up to him, and I mentioned how I went to one of their practices in '04. He laughed and said he was probably in trouble. He was right, because he and Langford were about to fight.)

There wasn't a huge need for me to take an official visit to Kansas because it was so close and I was there a lot. The coaches didn't force the issue for me to take a visit because they saw me all the time. Who knows, maybe they knew it was a slam dunk for me to end up at KU.

"We didn't want to take Travis for granted. You could tell, based on things he could do on the court at an early age, that he was special. But just because he was in Kansas City, we couldn't assume he'd come to Kansas. Having a player nearby helps a lot, but sometimes it's a hindrance. It depends on a lot of the influencing factors. For us, getting a chance to see Travis play in high school and on the AAU circuit, we felt good that he was in our backyard, but there are no guarantees in recruiting at all. Coach Self talked about, over and over, that Travis needed to feel how much we wanted him as part of our program. I'm glad we were able to do that."

— *Danny Manning*

I remember being at Late Night and sitting between the Morris twins. I tried my best to talk to them and get to know them. They were incredibly quiet. That experience might've made them a lock for Kansas. I don't see how any kid, who loves the game of basketball, could come to Late Night and not want to play at a place like that. If you're a kid who's experienced Late Night before, it's one thing. But to see how crazy the crowd is for the first "practice" of the season, I don't know how you couldn't go to a school that's not all about that.

After that first experience with Late Night at Allen Fieldhouse in 2004, I kept returning each October. In fact, when counting my five years in school, I went to Late Night 10 straight years.

Before suiting up for the Jayhawks, I had a full year of basketball to play, including a final season at Miege with Trevor.

Trevor has made highlight-reel passes for the University of Alabama, but he had impressive ones at Miege, too. One play that stands out was at Blue Valley, and Trevor was going in on a fast break lay up. A big guy was trailing him, which Trevor knew, so he just dropped the ball off behind him, I grabbed it without missing my stride and dunked it over the big guy.

Trevor knows how to create for himself and others. Even though it didn't seem like it, he always has his head up. He makes everyone around him better. That's why I think it would've been real nice if he had come to Kansas. He was recruited as a last-minute deal. By the time KU contacted him, he had his mind set on Alabama. That was around the same time KU was going after Josh Selby. Hey, coaches make recruiting mistakes sometimes.

With Trevor running the point, and then adding Willie Reed, who played in the league with Memphis, Jason Payton, Justin McKay and me to the mix, our Miege teams pressed, and got up and down the court. We loved to score. We didn't have many guys coming off the bench so there wasn't a lot of subbing. I never came out for more than a minute or so and Trevor never came out during my senior year (his sophomore season). Coach Zych never made us run in practice because we were constantly running in games and never getting tired.

The DiRenna Award

At the end of my senior year, I was selected as the Player of the Year for a second time in the EKL (Eastern Kansas League), and I was a finalist for the DiRenna Award, which is given each year to the top high school player — boy and girl — in the Kansas City area.

I was up for it after my junior year, but my AAU teammate and future fellow Jayhawk, Conner Teahan, won it, which wasn't surprising. He was having huge games, scoring more than 30 six times, and hitting buzzer beaters and Rockhurst finished second in Missouri Class 5. I was the youngest kid in the finalist group, so I didn't really have a shot at winning.

My senior year, though, I felt I had a decent chance. Dominique Morrison from Raytown, who ended up going to Oral Roberts, had five 30-plus point games and two games with more than 40. I didn't know how I'd compete with him. Johnny Coy from St. Joseph Benton, who ended up playing baseball at Wichita State, was a finalist. Great players. Still, I had won some big postseason awards — All-American (junior and senior years), Kansas Gatorade State Player of the Year, Kansas Player of the Year — so I felt the DiRenna was a possibility.

Much to my surprise, Marcus Denmon from Hogan Prep, who went on to play at Missouri, won it. I couldn't believe it! I'm not saying I should've won it, but Marcus wasn't high on my list to win it. Marcus was a great player and was scoring a lot of points, but there were other guys having bigger seasons. We actually played Hogan Prep early in the season at our place and I got the best of Marcus and their team, so I would've expected to have the upper hand on him for the DiRenna. (He had 29 points and I had 33 in our 73-58 win.) Again, he's a great player, but there were other guys who would've been less shocking winners.

> *"When I think back to our days at Miege together, the one game that stands out the most is when we played Hogan Prep in a Kansas-Missouri showdown. People were talking a lot about Marcus Denmon, and Travis took that to heart. That was a different Travis on the court that day. He definitely was the best one that day."*
>
> *— Trevor Releford*

A couple years after me, in 2010, I started to think the voters didn't like the name Releford. If there was a slam dunk for the award, it had to be Trevor in 2010. Miege went 25-0 with him at the point, and he was scoring a ton of points. Instead, it went to Daylen Robinson, who went to a smaller school, Northeast, and didn't accomplish as much as Trevor. I was hot after that — much more so than me not winning it. You have to give the award to the top guy on the best team, at least you should. I guess the voters didn't see it that way.

Closing out AAU with a great honor: USA Basketball

The summer after my senior year, not only was my last time playing AAU ball, but I had a unique chance to play on the USA

U18 National Team that won the silver medal at the 2008 FIBA Americas U18 Championship in Argentina.

When you play in the big AAU tournaments, you're playing in front of scouts for USA Basketball, for various scouting services, plus scouts for the Adidas and Nike camps, and camps that are run by NBA players. For instance, that summer I got to attend the Steve Nash Camp, which had a bunch of NBA scouts watching.

Participating in the process for USA Basketball was incredible. We had a two-week tryout, of sorts, in Washington, D.C. The first week featured more tryouts and running drills. The second week was tryouts to determine who'd go to Argentina.

Our head coach was Bob McKillop, Davidson's head coach. Anthony Grant, who's now Trevor's coach at Alabama, was one of the assistant coaches, as was John Thompson III from Georgetown. Our team included Kemba Walker, who went to UConn; Malcolm Lee, from UCLA; David and Travis Wear, the twins from UCLA; JaMychal Green, who played at Alabama; Mason Plumlee, who went to Duke; and Maalik Wayns, who played at Villanova.

That was an incredible experience that seemed to go by way too fast. We were in Argentina for about a week, but we only practiced and played in scrimmages for the first few days, and then we got into tournament play.

Through being seen at AAU tournaments, basketball gave me the chance to attend an Adidas camp in Shanghai, and another camp in Frankfurt, Germany. It's funny to think about that one now because I played on the same team there as Jeff Withey. You learn quickly in college that playing against those top guys in various tournaments, you're bound to see them again within the next four years.

While I was playing in these tournaments and getting ready to head to Lawrence, rumors were flying that Bill Self was going to leave Lawrence and become the head coach at Oklahoma State. Of course, the main people starting those rumors were

Self haters, Oklahoma State folks and members of the media who wanted to stir the pot.

The NCAA already had its rule that if the coach was leaving you were stuck going to the school where you signed the scholarship, so there wasn't much I could do if Coach Self left. I was worried, but only slightly. I didn't see how he'd leave after winning the national championship, even if it is his alma mater, Oklahoma State.

People think Oklahoma State is a tough place for opponents so it'd be tough for him to turn down the money and his alma mater. The only time it's that wild in Gallagher-Iba is when they play Kansas and probably Oklahoma. It's not like playing a game at Allen Fieldhouse, where even our exhibition games are crazier than other teams in the league. When we show up, our fans have the best signs that they've been thinking about all summer. That's why you go to Kansas — to play in that environment. To play in those games. To have that target on your back.

The decision to play at Kansas, for me, was based on both Coach Self and KU. I picked both, definitely.

Some kids go to the school to play the style that coach teaches. If that coach leaves, another coach comes in who might play a completely different style that doesn't suit a certain player. So, with the way the NCAA has the rules set up, you're expected to pick a school because of the school and not the coach. That's not realistic.

Since you can't go straight to the NBA, guys with dreams of playing in the league are using college to get noticed, of course. If the coach who recruited you because you fit his style (and vice versa) leaves for another job, the NCAA should allow you to get out of your commitment. Even if they say you can't follow that coach to the new school, going to a program that fits your style is better than staying in a bad situation.

Let's say Coach Self did leave in 2008 and KU hired a guy who plays 100 percent zone defense and shoots a lot of 3s. I'd be stuck and I might not be playing professionally right now. Thankfully, we don't have to worry about that because Coach Self turned down Oklahoma State.

And I was about to begin my career as a Jayhawk.

4 Finally a Jayhawk

There are three truths that every freshman basketball player at the University of Kansas won't understand until he's there.

One... you'll work harder than you've ever worked.

Two... you'll get chills every time you run through the tunnel at Allen Fieldhouse and into a gym with 16,000 of the loudest, most incredible fans you've ever imagined.

And three ... Coach Bill Self loads up on a bunch of players that he thinks can win a national championship, but he plays only seven guys in the regular rotation.

I'll explain.

Truth: you'll work harder than you've ever worked.

Freshmen are expected to work summer camps at KU, which, besides giving us a chance to meet some of our teammates and be around the coaches, we can start to get into the grind of college classes.

All of the freshmen had to report for the first session of summer school, which helped. When we got there, our days were pretty much planned for us from the time we woke up until the time we went to bed. After the first few months of being there, you get used to managing your time. The first few months are rough, though, unless you're used to waking up, going to classes, followed by practices, tutoring and then studying. People didn't like it, but the schedule got easier each year.

At first, I thought the practices were tough because they were four hours long. Getting used to the amount of time and adjusting physically and mentally was tough. Then, throw classes on top of that, and it makes for a full day.

We learned quickly that Coach Self has structured practices but sometimes he strays off the plan. Sometimes we'd do drills longer or shorter than he'd planned, depending on how the day was going.

Truth: you'll get chills every time you run through the tunnel at Allen Fieldhouse and into a gym with 16,000 of the loudest, most incredible fans you've ever imagined.

Before our first game of the season, at Allen Fieldhouse against UMKC, I was nervous, to say the least. Even though we had a better team, there was a lot of pressure because we didn't want to come out and lose to UMKC. And then there's the tunnel. Every former player talks about "the tunnel."

Coming out of the tunnel for the first time is indescribable. Nerves are running through your body, the crowd is going absolutely crazy, while the band blares "I'm a Jayhawk." I'm getting

The freshman nerves went away during our first game against UMKC. This is how I pictured my freshman year: me on the court, possibly leading a fast break.

chills thinking about it now. Seven of us on the 2008-09 squad hadn't experienced that before. Coach told us before the game that we'd be nervous but once we got in and started playing, the nervousness would go away. He was right, but that electric feeling of running into the Fieldhouse before the starting lineups never leaves a player.

Truth: Coach Bill Self loads up on a bunch of players that he thinks can win a national championship but he plays only seven guys in the regular rotation.

This was the hardest fact for me to learn and then to swallow as a freshman, especially with the way my career started at KU. In August 2008, just a few months after the Jayhawks won the national championship against Memphis and many of those players left, the 2008-09 team went north for a "Tour of Ottawa" — three exhibition games against three schools in Canada. We won the three games against McGill University (72-67), Carleton University (84-83) and the University of Ottawa (95-60).

That trip was awesome. Coach told us ahead of time that it wasn't competition like we'd be facing during the regular season, but it was a way for us to see another part of the world and, more importantly, get our competitive juices going against someone other than our teammates.

Sherron Collins was hurt and the twins, Marcus and Markieff Morris, weren't on the trip. I ended up leading the team in scoring with 11, 25 and seven points, respectively, in the three games. Heading back to Lawrence, my confidence was sky high. I just knew that I was going to be one of the main go-to guys.

As soon as we got to campus and started playing real games, the trip to Canada didn't seem to matter. Since I wasn't in the seven-man rotation, I was constantly looking over my shoulder when I was on the court, afraid that if I did something wrong I'd be pulled out of the game. That's how I played my first two seasons. Some guys had longer leashes than others. I was on a short leash. Tyshawn Taylor would mess up and not worry about coming out. When I was coming off the bench, if I messed up, I knew I was coming out. I played out of fear those first two years.

To Coach Self's credit, he trusts the older guys a lot more. It's not too often he has freshmen come in and run the show like other schools. He teaches you the way he wants you to play and then you have to earn his trust. It sucked because I could do what the guy in front of me was doing, but Coach didn't see it that way throughout the season. We had eight guards that year with Brady Morningstar, Tyrel Reed, Sherron, Tyshawn, Conner Teahan, Tyrone Appleton, Mario Little and me, but only four played. He tells every team before the year that he's going to play only seven guys regularly, and that the eighth and ninth guys would get in but they wouldn't be happy with their minutes.

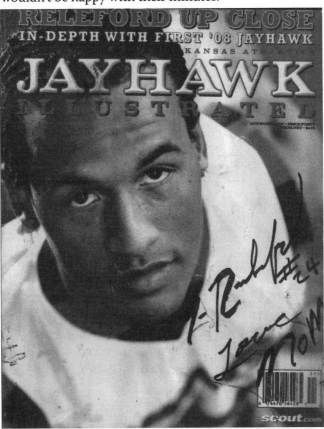

Shortly after I committed to Kansas, Jayhawk Illustrated wanted to do a story on me as the first in my class. Funny but I also ended up being the last one to leave.

That really bothered me at first. Who am I kidding? It bothered me a lot and for most of my freshman season. Coming in, all of us were top guys in our cities and on our AAU teams. We were highly recruited. I thought I'd play right away because most of the team — the 2008 national title team — was gone. I wasn't happy at all because I felt I could've been out there helping. We were winning, though, so it was hard to be mad at Coach Self. Unless we started losing my playing time wasn't going to change. It's easy to look back now and say how my freshman year was one in which I continued to work hard and get better, and how I took that year to do my best to be a good teammate and learn, and be the best first guy off the bench. Sure, I can say all of those things now, but at the time, it was brutal. It's not why I came to Kansas. I came to play and help contribute to championships.

"Travis was always going to be a kid that would do anything we asked him to do. He could learn easily, it's just that we had guys ahead of him that were older. You don't just play guys to play them. Travis won't want to hear this, but we did not recruit Travis for his freshman year or even his sophomore year. We recruited him for what we thought he could become, especially after he tightened up a few things. We do that with all the kids we recruit. I think projecting is probably more important than evaluating. We certainly have had a lot of success with some really good kids that have come in, paid their dues and next thing you know they get better and they end up being really good players. I think it is humbling for kids, though, because they go from being a star to a situation where they may not contribute in a way that they had imagined themselves contributing. But by no means was that a negative with us in recruiting Travis. We recruited him for what he could be, and he probably played out to be a little better than what we expected. Travis was, without question, a highly

*recruited kid that we knew we had to have. We're
lucky that we were able to get him."*

— Bill Self

Along with that seven-man rotation, there's the idea that not every player Coach Self recruits stays at KU, let alone breaking the top seven.

My first year those guys were Tyrone Appleton and Quintrell Thomas. Neither one turned out to be the player that Coach Self thought they'd be. Both guys played fewer minutes and in fewer games than me. That's one of those situations where you can't fault Coach Self for bad recruiting — the guys just didn't quite fit the system the way it appeared they might.

Throughout the non-conference part of our schedule, I wasn't seeing a ton of minutes. I had played 13 to 15 minutes a game against teams like UMKC, Coppin State and Albany, and I made the most of those minutes usually, but it wasn't what I expected to be playing. I logged 21 minutes against Michigan State in our first "real" road game — besides Arizona — before conference play. That was most court time I'd see all season. Unfortunately, I missed both shots I attempted, along with two free throws.

My frustration kept mounting and might've peaked after we played Missouri in Columbia on Feb. 9. Most importantly, we lost the game, 62-60, which was incredibly disappointing. Besides Missouri being our biggest rival, it's especially tough for a kid from the Missouri side of Kansas City. Their fans were crazy and mean. They were waiting for us when our bus pulled up. They were cussing and flipping us off when the bus got there. They even threw some rocks at the bus! When we got to the court, we wanted to bury the Tigers. Instead, they hit a shot that beat us.

Missouri was the craziest place to play. As I learned that season, right behind Missouri were Kansas State, Iowa State and Oklahoma State. At every other place, I thought we had more fans than the opponent. In Colorado the whole upstairs was blue. It was Allen Fieldhouse West, as they called it. At the start of the game, you can hear them cheering for us and booing the Buffaloes. By the end of the game we could easily hear the "Rock Chalk Chant," which is a wonderful sound.

I played eight minutes and scored nine points in that game against Missouri, which was my highest point total of the season. That game was my style of play: getting up and down, and making fast-reaction plays. In those nine minutes, I hit three of four shots and was 3-for-3 from the free throw line. All three buckets from the field were layups.

At that point, I thought I should've been playing more. Instead, my minutes went down for the next couple games.

"We'd have some conversations, even when he was at Kansas. I think Travis is so focused on doing everything to please a coach. He felt like his role with Coach Self was to be a defensive guy off the bench, so he was going to perfect that. Throughout his career he was the defensive guy who made sure the ball was getting to the right places. He was more aggressive during his senior year. When you get away from things you're good at, you forget to use it. He was comfortable making the right plays. Occasionally he'd show that he could score, but he saw his role at Kansas as more of a defensive guy. He took special pride in his defense. He loved to guard the other team's top player. He wants to win, which makes him a good teammates. He knows to win you have to stop the other team from scoring. It's unique because not a lot of kids buy into that. He hung his hat on that."

— *L.J. Goolsby, AAU coach*

One game that really stands out from that season was a "Big Monday" at Oklahoma on Feb. 23. It was an important game because, even though they were ranked No. 3 in the country and we were 15th, we were tied with the Sooners in the Big 12 standings. Plus, they had a 19-game winning streak at home, which is always fun to break.

RELENTLESS

Willie Warren was a big-time freshman for Oklahoma that year. He was from Texas, but we faced each other throughout our AAU careers, going back to middle school. He hit some big shots that game and ended up with 23 points. He had their crowd going crazy. But Willie made a big mistake: he started talking trash after making a few shots over Sherron. That's all it took. Sherron became a completely different player and took over in the second half. He couldn't miss. Coach was calling plays for Sherron and letting him run what he wanted to run.

Sherron scored 26 points, with 22 of them in the second half. Ty had 26, also, which was a career-high for him. I can't leave Cole Aldrich out. He scored 15 and had 20 rebounds!

We won, 87-78, which gave us a one-game lead over Oklahoma and Missouri in the Big 12.

I can't say enough great things about Sherron. He carried the team our whole freshman year. When things weren't going our way, we'd look at him to get things going. Coach did the same thing.

Off the court, Sherron was huge for me that year. He was the person who helped me the most in dealing with the frustration I felt. He knew who I was coming in as a freshman, and he saw how hard I worked in practice and how frustrated I was getting. He kept telling me to keep working hard and be ready when my time came. Look at his career. He didn't play early, or didn't start until his junior year. He could've gone to any school and started but he stuck with KU. He was more than willing to be a sounding board, and I knew I should listen to him because he had gone through it.

With our newly established one-game lead in the conference, we hosted Missouri at Allen Fieldhouse in our next game, on March 1. We were terrible hosts. To put it nicely, the game was ugly.

When we looked at the stat sheet from the first game, we figured there was no way we should've lost. We knew we had them, we just needed to play our game. We didn't want them to think they could play with us. Our fans were crazy the whole game, which gave us a lot of energy throughout the game. In the past when we're up big, you could tell we weren't in it as much. That Missouri game, we wanted to beat them by 100. We didn't quite do it, but a 25-point margin, 90-65, isn't bad.

I still don't like them.

In spite of the blow out and playing 10 minutes at Oklahoma, I didn't play any longer against the Tigers. In fact, I played only five minutes in that game. Of course, I wasn't happy but, again, we were winning so Coach Self couldn't be faulted. He had found the seven-man rotation that worked for our team.

The rotation worked so well that we held our lead in the conference and ended up winning the regular-season championship. We got our rings and continued our streak. Coach stresses the conference championship every year, and with every year the Jayhawks win, the tougher it'll get for the next team because every Big 12 opponent wants to knock us off. After every practice, one of the things we chanted was "Big 12 champs." That'll continue. That's one of the team's main goals going into the season.

Our other goal, of course, is the national championship. We didn't repeat as champs in 2009. Our season ended on March 27 with a 67-62 loss to Michigan State in the Sweet 16.

After we lost that game, we constantly heard from fans who told us how proud they were because, even though we had a whole new team from 2008, we still won the Big 12 conference championship. It was exciting to think that we had the whole team returning for 2009-10. I wasn't happy about my playing time but the fans were proud of us, which is a huge bonus of being a Jayhawk.

As far as my playing time, I barely touched the court in our three NCAA Tournament games. After not playing against North Dakota State in our first game, I knew I wasn't going to play much during the rest of the tournament, but I was ready. (I'm credited with playing one minute in the NCAA Tournament — against Dayton in the second round.)

Maybe the writing was on the wall. I started wondering why I came to KU. Family members were telling me to go somewhere else. I came in feeling like I could play right away with the guys that we had, but not getting a chance as a freshman made me wonder if this was the right place for me. That feeling only deepened in the upcoming months.

The X-Factor in Taking a Redshirt

Any excitement and visions I had of playing more during my sophomore year vanished right before the season started.

With the signing of Xavier Henry, who was a great freshman, I might've been able to see that there was a chance I'd be the odd man out. Coach Self met with me and said something I never expected to hear: "You can play this year or you can redshirt. If you play, your playing time will be like your freshman year or less because we have a lot of guys. If you redshirt, you can look at the plus side that you have a year to work on your game, get better and come back next year to be a three-year starter."

Coach added that he didn't want me to transfer, which is something I considered for a few days. In the past, guys have left Kansas because of that same conversation. In some of those conversations, Coach has suggested that they might not fit the program. He wasn't telling me that. He said he had confidence in me but the timing wasn't right and that I wasn't quite ready.

As he was saying all of this, I was stunned. I never imagined going to school to redshirt — or go an extra year. Or did I want to be the type of player who left Kansas and went to a smaller program? After all, most of the guys who have that conversation with Coach Self don't end up leaving Kansas for a school that's as prominent.

I told him I'd have to think about it.

As Coach's words sunk in during the next few hours, I was both disappointed and mad. I questioned my ability and tried to figure out what I was doing wrong. I felt like I was doing things to prove that I could be on the court but it wasn't what Coach had planned at the time. It was tough.

For a few days, the thought of transferring was very tempting, mainly because of Trevor, who was a senior at Bishop Miege. He hadn't decided on a school yet, so I thought we might be able to find a school that would take both of us. It would've been cool to try to play a few more years with him. I felt that schools would take us because we'd played together before. Look at Kansas; they were taking Xavier and his brother, C.J.

> *"It was cool to think about the possibility of playing with him again in college, if he had transferred somewhere, but Travis loves KU so much that he wasn't going to leave. I think we all knew that at the end of the day, he'd stay at Kansas and use that year to get better."*
> — *Trevor Releford*

I sat out the exhibition games to consider my options. That's when I decided I wanted to stay. I wanted to prove everyone wrong. Coach had confidence but I wanted to show that I could play a big role for Kansas. Plus, these guys were brothers to me and I didn't want to go somewhere else and try to create that bond. The fans were great throughout the process, which was big, too. I was getting plenty of fan love. So, I got after it every day in practice.

> *"Without question, I wanted him to stay. As he says, I told him that he could play (and not redshirt) but I didn't think he'd beat Xavier out. I said, 'If you can't beat him out, you know he's likely to be gone in a year, so why wouldn't you want a chance to start here a couple years instead of starting here one year?' I told the media when he really hadn't played at all that he'd score 1,000 points for us. He didn't, but he ended with 965. If we hadn't blown a big lead*

*(against Michigan in the 2013 NCAA Tournament),
he might've gotten there."*

— *Bill Self*

*"I was in Walmart when someone started talking
about how Travis Releford was redshirting. I asked
a lady what that meant because I hadn't heard
the term before. I was not happy because I thought
Travis had done something wrong and was losing
his scholarship. He tried telling me that it wasn't
a bad thing, but I didn't believe it until I talked to
Mr. Self and he said he wanted Travis at KU, but he
wanted Travis to sit out and improve. When Travis
told me he was thinking about leaving, I said, 'No,
you picked that school and you're going to stay
there.' As long as he wasn't getting kicked out, I was
fine, which meant Travis needed to stay."*

— *Venita Vann*

*"He was my roomie, so I was just trying to keep him
positive. At that time I was going through my own
stuff, but I was trying to keep him mentally tough.
Once he decided he wasn't going anywhere, that
Kansas is where he wanted to be, I was happy and
relieved. We were friends and roomies for about a year
already, so I didn't want him to go anywhere. I knew
how frustrated he was not to be playing but he stuck
it out. I'm happy he did for my own selfish reasons,
just to have my guy around. It was a tough situation
for him but I think he handled it pretty well. I think
he took it as a challenge. I think he wanted to prove
to everybody that he was just as good as everybody
else that was playing. Travis ended up having a pretty
good career afterwards, so it worked out."*

— *Tyshawn Taylor*

Looking back now — and even at the time — that year was

the most fun I had as a college player because it was stress free. I felt I could've been out there helping our team, but at the same time I was having a blast. There was no pressure. I'd go to practice and give my teammates the business and then I'd hang out with friends who weren't on the team. Most of the guys at Kansas hung out with only guys on the team, but I branched out early and was friends with kids in the classroom, old friends from high school and even some football players.

Practicing that year with the team gave me confidence that I could compete with guys who were going to be NBA players, namely Xavier. Coming in, he was bigger and stronger than the other guys in his class. He could shoot and was athletic. But when we were playing each other, the majority of the time, I'd have the best of X and the other guys in front of me. They had trouble

Once I knew the parts of my game that needed work, I had a blast during my redshirt season. I wanted to be playing, of course, but it was fun going against Xavier Henry (left) and Sherron Collins (center) in practice. Sherron was a huge help during my first couple years at KU. He really took me under his wing and helped me get through a tough situation.

scoring on me. I just stuck it out and competed. Of course, I was always talking trash to them. I was on the red team and whenever I did something in practice, I made sure they knew it. I was always the guy talking smack. So, even though the redshirt sucked at first, after awhile my game improved. I saw myself getting better and getting my confidence back. The game was fun again.

"Travis is an incredible competitor and he's very confident. He's so confident in his ability that if you ask him, he'd probably tell you that he was the best shooter and best passer on the team, and he always wanted to prove that. In his redshirt year, the practices were his games. So, he came to practice every day with that mindset, excited to be out there. Guys would be complaining about having to go to tutoring and being tired or whatever, but Travis came ready to play, with a smile on his face, every day. We'd be going home from practice and I'd be complaining about Coach Self or whatever, and it'd hit me that Travis wasn't playing and he was frustrated, but he wasn't complaining. He probably felt like he got the short end of the stick, but he loved to be there. The thing I'll always respect about Travis is how, in the time I was with him, he had a lot of stuff going on away from the court, but he was an incredibly positive person.

"Trav probably doesn't know how much I learned from him in his whole mentality and the way he carries himself. He's the type of person you just want to be around because his attitude is always positive. I respect so much that you can't really shake him up and cause him to have a bad day. He's going to be who he is regardless of what's going on around him. I learned so much about myself from him. We came from similar backgrounds and our moms became close and stayed with each other in Lawrence. So, coming from where we came from and seeing the things that each of us saw

growing up, I learned how to enjoy every moment, take it as it is, and learn from it."

— *Tyshawn Taylor*

The only time I had to worry about the scouting report that season was in practice. The coaches would have me play like a certain upcoming opponent. Usually, I was playing the part of the guy that shot all the time. Maybe that's part of the reason the game was fun again.

I remember dunking on Tyrel something crazy in practice one day. There was a scramble play. I beat Sherron to it, threw it behind my back, and then went and got it and slammed it over Tyrel's head. Believe me, I let them know a redshirt just did that. When you get dunked on, everyone reminds you of it in the locker room after practice. As the one doing the dunking, you definitely don't forget those moments.

"Travis is nice to everybody, but he has an ornery streak. And that ornery streak is what makes him good."

— *Bill Self*

Our red team was great. It was me, Mario Little, Jeff Withey, T-Rob and a point guard. The blue team had problems with us. I remember one time Sherron made a comment in an interview about how well the practice team prepares the starters. He said the red team would be second in the conference. I think we could've won the conference. There were days when they'd get really mad and give us problems. Remember, we didn't have rules. No fouls were called on us, while they had to play by the rules. We usually didn't play with plays, but we did that year. That's another reason it was so easy for me to want to stay. Even when I wasn't playing, I was having so much fun. But it bothered me at game time when I was sitting on the bench.

"That was a team that was fun to go to practice with every day. The starters knew they'd have to strap it on and bring it every day. Those teams are fun to be a part of, especially when Coach Self talks about possessions,

because you push guys to the top of their ability. Travis helped spearhead that. In his own way, he's a motivator on the court. With he and Mario Little redshirting that year, they were hungry. When you take a redshirt year you can work hard and use it to your advantage, or not work hard and lose some. Travis took it as a challenge to guard the better players on our team. He felt that he could guard, slow down and even stop some of the best players on our team. Then, when Travis started playing big, quality minutes, he was our defensive stopper. His mindset and desire made that redshirt year work out. That doesn't happen too often. A lot of times, guys transfer because they don't want to fight through adversity. Travis fought through it for himself and for his teammates because he wanted to see them do the best they could do. That gave guys extra motivation because you feel that you have to keep up with this guy. Travis brought that to the table every day for five years."

— Danny Manning

"I think that's what made our team so good, because every day in practice we came and competed against guys who could've been the starting five at most other schools. We competed like game situations with guys who could be starters on that KU team easily and for sure on different teams. So that made our team that competitive and that much better. I agree with Sherron about the red team. In my sophomore year — Travis's redshirt year — and junior year, we had 10 guys who could be interchangeable. You could sub a complete five out and the talent wouldn't drop off at all. I think that's why we were one of the best college teams in those two years."

— Tyshawn Taylor

As a redshirt, you don't have to travel to the away games.

That was fine with me because I don't like flying at all. Generally, I was on campus or at home in Kansas City when the team traveled. One road trip I chose to make was to UCLA in early December. I just wanted to go out and experience it. They went out a few days before the game and got to meet NBA Hall of Famer Jerry West — some of you might know him better as the guy who's used for the NBA logo. We met him when we went to dinner at some guy's house. Although calling this place a house would be the same as calling Elvis Presley's Graceland just a house or the White House just a white house. He had a full-size basketball court, which is where a lot of the Los Angeles Lakers workout, along with a movie theater, a bowling alley and an arcade. And that was only in one half of the house. We didn't get to see the other half. Seeing that house alone made the trip worth it to me.

On the court at UCLA, we ended up beating the Bruins, 73-61. So seeing the team win definitely made it worthwhile to risk flying.

Our first loss against any team that year was at Tennessee on Jan. 10. We were No. 1 in the country and they were No. 15. The Vols had a strange week because four of their main players were going to be out because of injuries and suspensions. It shouldn't have been a close game. I was at Hooters watching the game with friends, which made it worse as the game went on because I could see everything the guys couldn't see, but there was nothing I could do about it. Tennessee won, 76-68. Their fans stormed the court.

Afterwards, Coach Self made a pretty telling comment to the media: "I don't know if Tennessee was a team until this past week. I don't know if Kansas is a team yet."

Ouch.

It must've worked. We began conference play three days later and beat Nebraska 84-72. The team lost only one Big 12 game that season, at the end of February at Oklahoma State.

The only other loss that year was the last game of the season, in the second round of the NCAA Tournament to Northern Iowa.

Ouch.

THE X-FACTOR IN TAKING A REDSHIRT

With that loss, the season ended with as much of a negative vibe as it started with, and with about as much negative press.

Right before that season began, there was a rift between the football and basketball teams. The story was blown way out of proportion. And it's been told incorrectly — or told only partially.

From what was being reported in the media, most people thought a football player and a basketball player (presumably Tyshawn) got into a fistfight over a girl, and Ty hurt his hand. Two parts of that are true: there was a girl involved at one point, and yes, Ty hurt his hand. But there was a lot happening in the day or so between those two events. Trying to connect those two dots is like reading the first and last page of CliffsNotes for the Bible and thinking you understand the whole book.

Yes, a girl was involved initially but the first blow up was over a guy thinking he was being disrespected. Frankly, I didn't understand it. Maybe the girl brought the problem up, but it became more about a guy disrespecting another guy.

The next night is where some of the confusion comes in. Most nights, we ate dinner at the Burge Union after practice. For some reason, X and I decided to order Chinese food and go to his room to chill and play video games. So, we didn't actually see everything transpire.

As we were hanging out, though, Jordan Juenemann came in, freaking out: "Did you guys hear what happened? There was a huge fight between (such and such) and (such and such)!" (Of course I'm leaving their names out.)

The general perception was that a football player and a basketball player got into a fight over a girl. That's not true. The first beef between the two players was squashed before the incident at the Burge. The two guys had already talked and were cool. The fist fight started without either of those guys. Supposedly, a football player came out of nowhere, after the drama was squashed, ready to fight. He squared up and, from what I've been told, threw the first punch. Our guy had to fight.

Tyshawn was there but it wasn't his fight. He wasn't beefing with the football player, but he got caught up in the middle of it. Since the basketball players were involved, he had to do something. If X and I had been there, we would've had to do something to defend our teammates.

During the skirmish, Tyshawn dislocated his thumb, which drew all of the attention to him. What really got him into trouble was when he tweeted about it, saying he was OK. The coaches and administrators weren't happy about that.

Of course, none of the coaches from either side were happy about any of it. Coach Self and the assistants were especially mad because they knew how it was going to play out once it hit the media — which is partially what Ty's tweet did, it alerted the media. Once the story got out, it blew up to be about us instead of the football player throwing the first punch. Since basketball is bigger at Kansas, the story was about us starting the fight.

"You guys have to walk away situations sometimes," Coach told us afterwards. "You have to make better decisions." At the same time he probably would've been mad if we'd just walked away.

Too much was made of it as far as the basketball team was concerned. I understand that we were going into that season ranked No. 1, so the easy story is how the No. 1 team in the country has guys breaking hands in a fight with another team at the school. Of course, they were going to make a big deal of that and run with it.

"That's one of the times Travis was most important to me because in that whole situation, a lot of the heat fell on me. Whether it was my fault or not doesn't matter because I was there, in that room, in that situation. Travis and Xavier had walked past us about 10 minutes before that, so I could've easily ended up going with them. Instead, I ended up in the middle of what was a bad situation. I got into a lot of trouble because of that and, I felt, my name was being slammed. When Trav and I talked about it in the room, and I'd be mad about what was happening

or by what was being said, Travis would say, 'What are you gonna do? You just need to roll with it and take your punishment. What's the worst that's gonna happen?' He kept saying that. He also told me that, 'You know, in two months people are going to forget about this when we're winning games.' He was right. After the summer was over and the season started, people didn't remember it."

— Tyshawn Taylor

The day after the Burge fight, they brought both teams together and chewed us out behind closed doors and left it at that. Athletic Director Lew Perkins definitely let us know what the coaches and administrators thought about everything. They changed it to where we didn't eat at the training table. The football team kept going there but we were fed in the locker room.

This wasn't a big basketball team bullying the football team or rivalry type of story or however some of the media made it sound. I was friends with Phillip Strozier, who was a defensive back from Kansas City, and this didn't affect us. He wasn't at the Burge that night either, so we just compared notes of what we knew. We both thought it was crazy, but it didn't affect whether we could be cool with each other.

After everything died down and we got into the season, the two teams became cool again — but still kept a little distance.

Even though I never thought I'd be a redshirt at Kansas, it might've done something else to change my life forever. Early that season I met a girl named Jennifer Covell. We exchanged numbers, but she was leaving the country the next day for a few weeks. We ended up emailing on a regular basis while she was gone. When she got back we started hanging out. Things got pretty serious pretty quickly.

We found out at the end of that school year that she was pregnant.

I don't remember the exact details of when she told me, but I do remember being completely stunned. I still had three full seasons of college basketball in front of me, and she was still in school.

At first, I told Tyshawn because he was my roommate and closest friend. He was shocked. When you're young, you think that having kids while you're in college is the end of the world. I knew I was going to have a huge amount of support around me from blood family to basketball family. Jennifer's family was very supportive.

"I was probably more shocked than he was when he told me Jennifer was pregnant. Obviously it wasn't planned, so it's shocking in that way. But it's such a blessing. That wasn't an ideal situation for him, but I have a son who was born not long after Trav's, so to see how Trav handled that whole time helped me get through my situation."

— Tyshawn Taylor

The decision, ultimately, was going to be Jennifer's, but I told her that I'd be there for her in whatever she decided. We looked at adoption opportunities and talked about whether we'd be together in the future. We talked about the type of parents we'd be. We tried to talk about everything possible for the future.

Growing up, her parents were split up and, obviously, my dad was in prison, so it's not like either of us had the "perfect" home life to fall back on. Those backgrounds were a huge factor for us wanting to keep the baby; at least my background was huge in my part of the decision. We both wanted that to change for our kid even though it was early in our lives.

After a lot of discussing, thinking, praying and stressing, she decided she wanted to keep the baby and not give him or her up for adoption.

Suddenly, as I hit the summer, I was excited about the opportunity on the court the following season. The coaches and I all saw improvement in my game. I was excited and ready to play. And, now, I knew that regardless of what happened on the court, I had the nervous anticipation of knowing my life was going to change forever during the next season.

Tracy (on the right) and I in matching sweaters and jeans.

I don't know much about this picture, including where it was taken. I'm guessing I was about 1 year old. I do know I looked happy.

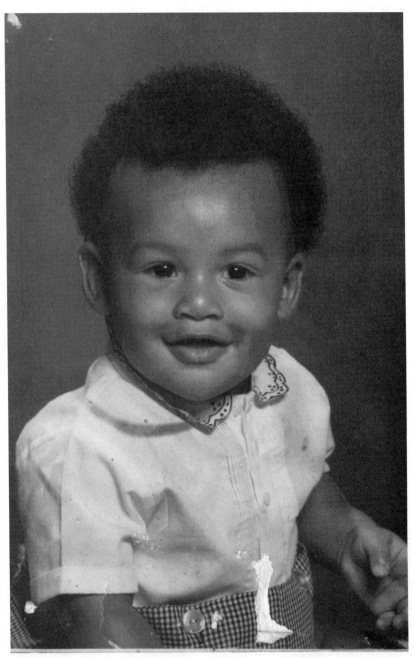

This is another one of those pictures that the best I can say is that I was probably 1 year old. And, again, I look happy.

Tracy and I in the middle of the floor at our house.

As kids, we were always with my uncle Walter (in the White Sox cap, holding Tracy), who I looked up to, and then my cousin Jason, who's holding me.

Another preschool picture. It looks like I'm reading a book or listening to one.

Trevor, cousin Arthur, Tracy, me and Tamara (sitting in front of Tracy) at Myrtle Beach, South Carolina. This was my first time at a beach. I was probably around the fourth grade.

I was probably about third or fourth grade in this picture. I had a snicker on my face because I'm sure I was forced to take the picture, and I definitely didn't want to take it. Or I was up to something. It was in the music room because I'll always remember the risers from that class.

Me, Tracy and cousin Arthur, who was like another brother. We were always together and all lived close. We stayed at each other's houses quite a bit growing up.

I played football for the Kansas City Seminoles in the eighth grade. Growing up, football was the first organized sport I played and one of my favorites to play. Eighth grade was my last year to play it, though. I will have to ask my mother why she trimmed these photos.

This was around Christmas in our side yard in the eighth grade. At the time, Carmelo Anthony and LeBron James were just getting into the league and gaining popularity. I received each player's jersey for Christmas.

Graduation Celebration
Travis Dwayne Releford
Tuesday May 25, 2004
Lee A. Tolbert Academy
3400 Paseo
Time 1:30 pm

My graduation announcement from middle school. One of my middle school year pictures. I was still a little ornery at this time in my life.

This was during an AAU tournament in Orlando, Florida. This fenced-in pool was at our house for the two weeks we were there. We were living in style. That was my last summer with the Magic.

From what I can remember, every time we went to an AAU tournament, they took a team photo and individual photos. This is one of those with the Magic, although I can't say where we were playing.

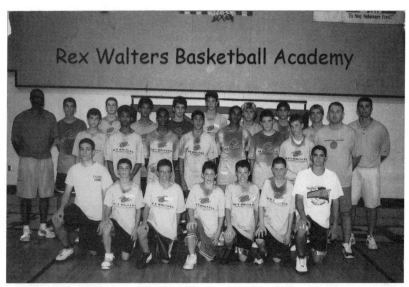

Rex Walters Basketball Academy was in middle school in Kansas City. I think it was at Blue Valley Northwest. I'm in the back row, fourth one from the left. Rex is in the back row on the far right. It's pretty cool to think now that Rex and I both played in a Final Four for Kansas.

Riley and I during an AAU tournament. Riley was a cool guy who always had a story to tell. The look on my face says that I didn't think his story was as funny as he thought it was.

This was with my grandma, Virginia Flowers, at a debutant ball during my senior year of high school. She played a big role in my life at an early age.

This was my senior year at Bishop Miege, getting ready for a game. By this time I'd already committed to Kansas and I was looking forward to a fun senior season.

This was a photo taken for the top players in the Eastern Kansas League. The girl is Tierra Ford. Bishop Miege had good boys' and girls' teams while I was there.

It's funny to see this picture now. This was when I first met Jeff Withey (tallest on right), when we played together on a team in Germany. We had a great time together, but little did either of us know that we'd end up playing together at Kansas a few years later.

This was the NCAA First Team program, which was somewhat of a mentoring program. The NCAA brought top high school athletes around the country, hand picked by NCAA First Team staff members, who were looking at talent, but also character on and off the court. We went through a camp, with guest speakers about being smart with your money and handling various pressures, and the NCAA rules. One of the speakers I remember the most was Charles Barkley. I was picked to go through the program three years. This was my senior year. (Trevor went through the whole program, too.) It was in a different city each year, which was a surprise — they'd let you know a few weeks before.

©Kansas Athletics, Inc., photographer Jeff Jacobsen

Our goal every year — as it will be as long as Coach Self is at KU — was to win the National Championship. One product of that has been the Big 12 title and a few Big 12 tournament championships. Here we are at the Sprint Center in Kansas City, Mo., after winning the 2013 conference tournament title.

©Kansas Athletics, Inc., photographer Jeff Jacobsen

With the combination of Kansas and Bill Self, I'm not sure how a recruit wouldn't pick the Jayhawks. Besides being an incredible coach, he's an even better person. I didn't fully understand Coach's system when I arrived at KU, but once I learned it and got to know him a little better, we had a great relationship. As I told him a lot during my last couple of years: "I know, Coach. Don't worry, I got this."

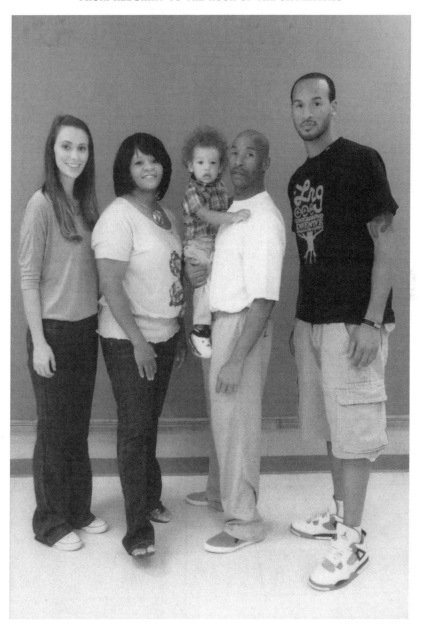

This was spring 2012, with Jennifer, TJ, and Mom, visiting Dad. This was the third or fourth time that Dad had seen TJ, but it was Mom's first time to see Dad in 15 years. Looking at this picture, it's a wonder that I got some height to play basketball.

I'll let TJ play whatever sports he likes growing up, but I don't mind "encouraging" him while he's young.

The weekend before moving to Belgium I was able to get together with my close friends in Kansas City.

This is at Maximiliaan, my favorite restaurant in Aalst. Here I am with teammates (from left) Ian Hanavan, Thomas Dreesen, Nicolas, who owns the restaurant, and Naim El Kounchar.

Talk about team bonding. We got to take a two-hour tour of Aalst on mopeds. And, no, I wasn't driving when I took the shot of myself.

Going in for a bucket in Belgium.

Freddy Van Geit for Okapi Aalstar

You know, in spite of the advertisements on the court and on our uniforms, basketball is just basketball. I'm blessed to be playing it professionally.

Freddy Van Geit for Okapi Aalstar

It's great to have Jen and TJ in Belgium with me. The Supercup, which our team won in September, is almost as big as TJ. That'll change soon enough, I'm sure.

I love working with kids. This one was taken while I was helping at Cole Aldrich's camp.

TJ and I hanging out — literally — at the park.

Hanging out with TJ, playing on the PS3. One of the fun things to do with teammates away from basketball — when studying is done, of course — is to play video games. TJ's getting an early start.

There's an uncanny resemblance, I guess, between TJ and me when I was about his age. It's cool that we happened to catch him when he was next to my picture.

6 Sophomore Year

This was going to be it: my sophomore season. The year I'd start more games and see more time on the court. Things were right on cue, too.

I started our first two games — Longwood and Valparaiso — and was playing nearly half of every game. I think that's when Coach decided I played better coming off the bench. That was true. When I came off the bench I provided a spark, which is what a player off the bench should do. I could make something happen.

After cruising through our first four games of 2010-11, we went to Las Vegas for games against Ohio and Arizona. In those two games, I came off the bench and was shooting lights out. In the first game against Ohio, I came off the bench and hit three 3-pointers in a row, and finished with what was then a career-high 13 points. The same thing happened with Arizona. They didn't want to play me as a shooter and I came out and hit two 3s, immediately. I scored 10 points against the Wildcats.

I was getting into a rhythm as a sub. Coming off the bench, I felt good about being the spark and providing instant offense. That's what I did with Arizona. From that game, I'll never forget the defender guarding me right in front of Arizona's bench, and an assistant coach yelling, "Back up, non-shooter; non-shooter!"

I made my first 3 and just stared at him. On the very next possession, I hit another 3 as they were yelling the same thing. Right after that shot I heard the head coach, Sean Miller, shout to his assistant, "I thought you said this guy couldn't shoot!"

The next time I got the ball, Arizona wasn't going to give me anything. "Get on him! Get on him! Don't let him shoot!" were the shouts from the coaches.

To their credit, before that I didn't shoot a lot from outside. Most of my points were in transition or driving to the basket. After the game, I was joking with my teammates that teams would have to change their scouting reports. I always had that confidence in my shooting. Coming out of high school I wasn't known as a shooter. It's not that I couldn't shoot, but I was bigger than everyone we played in high school. Why shoot it when you can go to the basket? In college, everyone was the same size and had the same athletic ability, so I had to get back to shooting more. After my junior season, I had all sorts of confidence in my shooting.

> *"The thing that amazed me about him is that when you are highly recruited at an early age, to be patient enough to understand that your time will come, is not an easy thing for kids now. Look at all these kids transferring, they all want to play right away. It's a very difficult thing to manage, but I think Travis handled it extremely well. It's not an easy thing to sit out a year and watch other people play. The way his career ended and the contribution he made to that program is pretty dramatic. It speaks volumes to his character."*
> — *Larry Brown, Hall of Fame coach*

We were seeing that we had a good team. Even though Sherron Collins was gone, we saw an incredible transformation in the Morris twins during the summer and early part of the season. They had a mentality that they wanted it to be their last year, so they busted it all summer. They were doing extra lifting, extra workouts, and going to the gym late at night. On top of that — with the help of Coach Danny Manning — their skill sets improved. Their work ethic was incredible, and it showed as they carried the team throughout the season.

I hadn't been around twins much before Marcus and Markieff, but it was fascinating to see them together. And there weren't many times you wouldn't see them together. They were together all the time off the court. They're probably like that now in the NBA since they're on the same team. They did everything together. You never saw one without the other. If you did, you had to ask where the other was because it was so odd. That's how they'd always been. They ate the same food, they lived together, and they had the same class schedule and tutoring schedule. Markieff was more chilled and laid back. Marcus was more outgoing. It took me awhile to tell them apart. I just called them "twins." Once you'd been around them enough you could see some differences, namely that one's a little taller than the other. They used to change jersey numbers in practice because coach couldn't tell them apart. That really messed him up, but he was cool enough to laugh it off.

As we got into the season more, my biggest motivator became Jennifer and our unborn son. Yes, we found out before he was born that he was going to be a boy. That's when I really started getting excited. Once we found out, we agreed to name him after me, largely because every first son in my family is named after his father. So he'd be Travis Jr., or TJ, for short.

Working hard to play professionally has always been my dream, but with a son on the way, it gave me another reason to work harder. Every time I didn't feel like doing a drill or lifting another rep in the weight room, I'd think about him and push harder.

Even though I didn't grow up with a father, per se, I wasn't nervous at all about being a dad. To this day, I think about how it's important for me to teach him what I know and what I've been through.

Originally, TJ was due on Jan. 10. I went with Jen to her doctor's appointment on the morning of Jan. 2. We found out TJ was ready. They decided to keep Jen at Overland Park Regional, but the doctor assured us that TJ wouldn't be born anytime soon.

RELENTLESS

That was a good thing because we had a game that night against Miami of Ohio. Thankfully, it was at Allen Fieldhouse.

Jennifer and I talked about what I should do. Once the doctor said that we had time, I decided to go to the game. I called Coach Self to let him know I was going to miss our shootaround because I was at the hospital. He was understanding, of course, and gave me the option of missing the game. I told him that it was going to happen later, so I was going to the game. It was a tough decision because I didn't want to miss my son being born, but I didn't want to let my teammates down.

Coach had to have known that night, though, that the one thing on my mind was what was happening at the hospital. I ended up playing only 12 minutes, mainly because I wasn't at shootaround, and missed all four shots I took.

As soon as the game was over, which we won, 83-56, I showered and got out of Lawrence as quickly as I could. I burned up K-10 and Interstate-435 to get to the hospital. Jennifer wasn't quite ready (or, I guess I should say TJ wasn't ready — Jen was ready!), so I had time to eat a postgame meal. As soon as I was done, it was time.

To put the next few minutes into words is nearly impossible. There aren't enough adjectives to describe the feeling of seeing your child being born. The first time I saw him, I was stunned. It was a little me! On top of that, as a lot of dads today can attest, I was the one who cut the umbilical cord. That whole night was just an amazing, unforgettable experience.

I was a dad.

As I write those words, I can't imagine life without TJ. Having him in my life has made me want to play harder, more focused and do all I can to play ball for as long as I can.

"Games are important but the birth of your first child probably trumps most games. If it'd been an NCAA Tournament game, I might've asked if (Jennifer) could delay things a little bit, but not this one. [Laughs.] He's been a good dad and I'm excited for his future

and his approach of how he's going to be the head of a family. I think he's got it figured out. But the birth of a child is one thing I don't think any coach should ever step in and say you can't miss a game, because that does trump everything."

— Bill Self

◆◆◆

Three days after TJ's birth, we played UMKC at Allen Fieldhouse. Usually this game wouldn't be such a big deal, but for me it was because my best friend, Mike Gholston, was playing

©Kansas Athletics, Inc., photographer Jeff Jacobsen

I've tried telling people that I had — and still have — bounce. This was a windmill dunk against UMKC during my redshirt sophomore year.

for the Kangaroos. Of course, we talked all the time, but there was plenty of trash talking leading up to that game.

One play that stands out was a time Mike was guarding me. I got a rebound and put up a shot over him. Coach Self got mad at me because I basically just threw the ball toward the rim. "Can't you take a better shot than that?!" he yelled. I missed the shot. Later, I was at the free-throw line, and he was the closest guy to me. He kept saying I was going to miss. After I made it, I held my hand out to him to shake it. His dad was in the crowd and said, "Look at Trav trying to give Mike a high-five."

We beat the Kangaroos that night, 99-52. I had another decent game with 13 points in 18 minutes.

Up next was Michigan, at their place. Even though I'd been playing more, after sitting out two years I still felt that if I messed up I was going to get taken out. That set me back, I think. You can't play well if you're timid or worried about screwing up. On top of that, a few minutes into my time on the court at Ann Arbor, I went up to block a shot, got a few inches off the ground and came down wrong. I badly twisted my ankle.

I sat out a few practices and missed the first five conference games, which started with Iowa State four days after the Michigan game. By the time I was ready to play, Coach had his seven-man rotation set.

One of the Big 12 games I missed was on Jan. 22, against Texas at Allen Fieldhouse. We were ranked No. 2 in the country and the Longhorns were No. 10. We were carrying a 69-game winning streak at Allen Fieldhouse. It seems as if that'd be a great game, a great weekend. Actually, that was a horrible weekend for our entire team, but not because of anything that happened on the court.

Every night before our games we'd have curfew and a late-night snack would be brought to the room. It was a room check, basically. Right before that, we were all downstairs, laughing and joking around. We went our separate ways until the next day. I was chilling in the room, watching TV, when Tyshawn came storming in: "Trav, Trav, come here" I could tell it wasn't good. "T-Rob's mom just passed."

We were stunned. We went down to his room and tried to comfort him, but what could we do or say? Shortly before that, he'd lost both his grandmother and grandfather. Now his mom? Lisa Robinson was young, but she apparently had a heart attack. Seeing T-Rob like that was incredibly hard. All we could do was cry with him. We wanted to be there for him, but we didn't know how to feel. It was a tough time.

We stayed up with him for awhile. None of us could sleep. The next morning, we had our walk through. We were all wiped out from the emotion and lack of sleep. Coach talked to us, saying that we needed to continue about our day and do our best to play the game. We didn't know if T-Rob was going to be there. Either way, we were going to play that game for T-Rob's mom.

Surprisingly, he played. As a team, fueled by adrenaline of the Allen Fieldhouse crowd and the desire to win for Thomas and his mom, the team played well in the first half. We were up 35-23 at halftime.

The locker room at half was unlike any we had during my five years at KU. It was completely quiet. Coach didn't say much; he just went over the stats.

But then staying up all night caught up with us in the second half. Texas played a great half, outscoring us 51-28. They went on to win the game, 74-63, and break our 69-game home winning streak. Basketball and the loss — or even a win — seemed so inconsequential at that moment. After the game we all started bawling again in the locker room, partially because we lost the game and let T-Rob down but mostly because of the hurt he was feeling, as if we could imagine that.

As a team, we wanted to be there for him at the funeral. The coaches did some checking and, in one of its more sane decisions, the NCAA cleared it for us to go as a team to the funeral. We all flew out to Washington, D.C., which was having a terrible snow storm. We shouldn't even have flown. It was so bad that we got stuck on the highway a couple of times. It was worth it, though, to be there for Thomas.

Coach was giving T-Rob time to be with his family, but he

wanted to be with us. That brought us closer. We were family. Suddenly, we wanted to win not only for our fans, our school and ourselves, but we wanted to win for T-Rob and his family. The games were different for him now. He couldn't go and call his mom as he would before. We desperately wanted to make it to the championship for him.

Thomas always worked his butt off, and he was a good guy, and then all of this stuff happens to him. God must have a crazy plan for this guy to have everything happen to him at once. It would've been very easy and understandable for T-Rob to leave after that season and try to play professionally, but he decided to stay another year and get better. He did that for himself and for us.

Two games after that Texas game, I was back in the lineup. Of course, the team had been cruising again with some big conference wins.

On Feb. 7, we hosted Missouri. I always looked forward to playing them. The rivalry games are the best games you play all year. That was true especially for a kid from Kansas City, Mo. — before Missouri left the Big 12. It's bragging rights all year. Since I'm from Missouri, I'd have to hear about it if we lost. And, believe me, since Missouri hasn't won anything in basketball, their fans definitely let me hear about their supposed "better team." The rivalry had such great history, going back to the Civil War times. I know Trevor's Crimson Tide have a great rivalry with Auburn, Duke and North Carolina have a heated one, Ohio State and Michigan have a big one, and KU's is good with K-State, but none of those compare, in my opinion, to Kansas and Missouri. It's a genuine dislike (read: almost hatred) for both sides. Coach Self reminded us of the history every time we played Missouri. Of course, most of the guys on the team didn't really understand it, but I did. Regardless, we tried to make the most of it.

The game was fast-paced with a lot of energy. Going into the game my confidence was high because it was an open-court, transition-type game. I thought it'd be good for me. It happened to play that way. I played 16 minutes, which was the most since the UMKC game a month earlier and was the most I'd play the rest of the season, and I did my best to take advantage of the time. I got a few easy baskets in transition and hit two 3-pointers. I ended the game with 10 points and three rebounds (all on the defensive end). We went on to cruise to a 103-86 win.

A week later, we played our other big rival, K-State, on Valentine's Day in Manhattan. The Wildcats definitely didn't show us any love. They were having a terrible year, but we went in there without anything on the game. Besides, we'd beaten them earlier in the season, 90-66, at home. They came in with a "this is our season" mentality and they beat us badly. From the opening tip they had crazy energy and we came out emotionless, as if it were just another game. They thumped us, 84-68. They didn't really change things from the first meeting; it was more of the effort on both sides. After the game, Coach didn't really get mad, but he knew we didn't give our best effort. In any game, he didn't necessarily care whether we won lost as long as we gave good effort. We disappointed him that night because of our effort, or lack of it.

Effort wasn't an issue again that season. We cruised through the remaining five conference games, including the regular-season finale at Missouri, which was the closest win, 70-66. We were, once again, Big 12 champs!

We put the finishing touches on a great season by winning the Big 12 Tournament in Kansas City. We beat Oklahoma State by one point (63-62) before taking care of business against Colorado and Texas. Unfortunately, it was déjà vu for me as I played only one minute in those three games. In fact, I played fewer combined minutes (10) in our seven postseason games than I'd averaged before getting hurt against Michigan (15-plus). But, again, we were winning so I wasn't going to — and didn't want to — rock the boat.

"Travis is a wonderful young man and an unselfish young man. Those are the two things that jump out right away when you talk about him. He has a wonderful personality where he's not necessarily

going to talk you to death, but you know being around him that he has a good heart. That quality comes out in how he carries himself."

— *Danny Manning*

I saw a lot of incredible dunks while playing for the Jayhawks, but this was my favorite dunk by one of my teammates. I had thrown the ball off the backboard for Elijah Johnson. He had some serious bounce!

We were beating up on everybody and we all believed that could be a year for us to win the NCAA Tournament. Really, out of the five years I was there, the only year we probably shouldn't have played for the national title was 2011-12, when we played Kentucky for the championship. But this season we had potential NBA lottery picks in the twins, along with strong guards.

The Selection Committee must've thought we were a pretty good team, too, because they gave us a No. 1 seed. Even though you play to put yourself in that position, there's more pressure when you're a No. 1. As a player, you feel like you have to go out and be No. 1 when you're ranked No. 1. As we've seen — and saw that season — any team in the tournament can win any given game. You have to go out with a goal to win one game at a time. Sometimes we looked ahead and sometimes we looked at numbers.

Our confidence was sky high because we had won the Big 12 regular season and tournament. We felt we were going to go beat up on teams we hadn't played all year. That's how it played out. We didn't struggle through the first three games: Boston University (72-53), Illinois (73-59) and Richmond (77-57). Incidentally, that Illinois game was the first time Coach Self had faced his old team since leaving for KU. Since it'd been almost 10 years since he left, we didn't hear much about Coach Self being at Illinois or all the stuff that Bruce Weber did when he took over as coach. All we really knew was that he had coached there and that the year Weber took them to the Final Four was with Coach Self's squad. Otherwise, there wasn't a lot of hype about the game.

Our next game, the Elite Eight, had some hype but only because we were playing a team in Virginia Commonwealth that had become a fan favorite. They were an underdog team as a No. 11 seed and they were fun for (some) people to watch.

We were confident that a couple hours after tip, we'd be celebrating a trip to the Final Four. We didn't feel we needed an excellent game. Obviously, that wasn't the case.

They hit about every shot they threw up, including four 3-pointers in a 13-2 run during the first half. The main guy hitting them was Jamie Skeen. As the game starts, if a guy's hitting everything, as a team you can't help but wonder if you should start packing up to go home. At halftime, VCU led 41-27.

As we'd heard and thought before in similar situations, Coach told us they couldn't keep shooting like that. Of course, they kept shooting like that. We weren't getting stops and they weren't missing shots.

People like to say we lost that game, 71-61, because of how VCU's coach, Shaka Smart, was a great coach and he out-coached Coach Self. Look, that was not the case — Coach Self did NOT get out-coached. VCU played 12 guys all year and kept putting guys in and out. They had an advantage because they had fresh guys every few minutes giving you different looks. We played seven guys. Players on both sides were making plays; they just made more.

Losing in the NCAA Tournament is always a bad feeling when you play for Kansas. Expectations that you place on yourself, let alone the expectations of the coaches and fans, make it a horrible feeling that sticks with you. Even though I hadn't played much since the injury against Michigan, guards Brady Morningstar and Tyrel Reed were seniors, so that would open two spots in the seven-man rotation. My junior season was going to be THE year...right?

7 Junior Year

In the first chapter of this book, I recounted the incredible NCAA Tournament run we had in 2011-12. Of course, there were a few other memorable games during the season that helped prepare us for the NCAA tourney.

For me, the preparation started for that junior season in earnest during the summer. Even with the departures of Tyrel and Brady, I decided that the best way to ensure more playing time was by working harder and getting better each day. I took more shots and made sure each day that I worked a little harder than the day before.

Once the season got started, we were tested early. Really early. After beating Towson State in our opener, we had a date with Kentucky at Madison Square Garden on Nov. 15. This game was huge because it was us and Kentucky on basketball's biggest stage — the Garden. We played Memphis there a year earlier, but the Kentucky game was different because there were more celebrity sightings. Spike Lee was there. Various actors. Carmelo Anthony and Chris Paul. It was crazy. That's when you realize, as a player, how big college basketball is to people. We all looked forward to playing in the Garden because of all the top guys in basketball history had had huge games there.

Wilt Chamberlain, Oscar Robertson, Dr. J, Michael Jordan and Kobe all have had big games in that building. It really felt like we were center stage on Broadway when they cut the lights out in the crowd, and the court was the only thing that was lit. What a feeling!

On top of that, to have two of college basketball's most storied programs there, made it a special night. Even though we'd heard countless times already how it was a "down year" for us because of all the talent we lost from the previous season, we felt confident that we'd beat Kentucky. Coach Self had beaten John Calipari and Memphis in the championship in 2008, so we liked the match up of coaches. Regardless, it'd be a good chance to see who we were as a team early in the season.

We played well in the first half; we just had a few things go against us. Looking at the stats, we had given them a bunch of points on their end and we missed a few layups and other easy buckets. Coach does a good job of adding that up and showing us that we could've been ahead if we'd hit those shots.

It didn't get better in the second half. In fact, things went downhill. Kentucky made things happen on both ends of the floor, and they beat us, 75-65.

Coach wasn't too upset afterwards. That type of game in November is more of a gauge to see where we are and see what we need to do to get better. It's so early that losing is not the end of the world. Besides, Kentucky had a good team, as everyone learned throughout that season. We knew we could've competed better but there was a lot of season left.

A week after being in cold New York City, we were hanging out on the beaches of Hawaii, as we traveled there for the Maui Invitational. It was a blast. We went over a few days before the games began to enjoy Hawaii. We had two practices, but the coaches let us enjoy the beach. It was a vacation and a business trip at the same time. Most of us had not been there, so the coaches didn't want to completely restrict us. And then, after the tournament, we had another day and a half to hang out. So, we definitely got plenty of time to hang out on the beach.

All three of the games during that trip stand out.

The first game we played was against Georgetown, which used the "Princeton offense" with a lot of backdoor cuts and 3-point shots. We changed our defensive scheme and how we guarded, and we kept up the intensity the whole time. It was a fun game that went back and forth. Thomas Robinson had a huge game for us with five or six monstrous dunks. He ended with a double-double, 20 points and 12 rebounds.

The game came down to the end. They hit one of their seven 3-pointers with about 30 seconds left, and cut our lead to two, 65-63. I was fouled with seconds left, and hit both free throws. That gave us the final score of 67-63.

I was beginning to feel really good about redshirting two years earlier, because the experience I gained that season was paying off, and Coach Self telling me that I'd have a chance to start for a couple of years was coming true. As was the case with every game that season, I started and was on the court most of the night. Looking back, in 29 minutes, I scored 10 points after going 4-for-4 from the field and 2-for-2 from the line, with four rebounds and a steal.

The next day we played another big-time school, UCLA. Our defense helped us grab a big lead early, and we were up by 19 at halftime. In the second half, we let up a little and the Bruins cut our lead down to five. But we wore them down and went on to win, 72-56. Coach wasn't too happy about that game because we could've played better. Luckily, he didn't have too long to get on us about it because we had Duke the next day for the tournament championship.

As expected, we went back and forth with No. 6 Duke the whole game in one of the best atmospheres for a college game outside of Allen Fieldhouse — or at least it was that night. The games were played in a very small gym, not noticeably bigger than our gym at Bishop Miege.

There was a great battle inside between Thomas Robinson

and Mason Plumlee. T-Rob ended the game with 16 points and 15 rebounds; Plumlee had 17 and 12.

As luck would have it, the game came down to a prayer of a 3-point shot by Tyler Thornton. With the shot clock running out

©Kansas Athletics, Inc., photographer Laura Jacobsen

Besides being a great teammate, Tyshawn Taylor is like a brother to me.

and about 20 seconds left in the game, Thornton hit a wild shot that gave Duke the lead. He didn't play much and he didn't shoot 3-pointerss, but he hit that one.

During the summer of 2013, while I was playing for the Denver Nuggets' summer league team in Las Vegas, I ran into Thornton. He knew it was a crap shot, but in case he didn't, I let him know it.

It didn't matter, the Blue Devils won, 68-61.

That was one of Tyshawn's worst games. He had 11 turnovers, which we were trying to overcome. He was mad at himself and others for not making plays. It wasn't all his fault, but it went down as his stats. He had a double-double, I guess, in points and turnovers. Coach gave him a hard time later about having a double-double in that game. It was definitely a learning process of how we did against another top team and another top coach. We were 3-2 after that game.

It was disappointing to lose — as it was any time we lost — but we couldn't be down on ourselves too much. Even Coach felt that way right after the Duke game.

"I can't imagine there being a better atmosphere than that game with two historic programs," he told ESPN after the game. "I know our guys had a blast playing in it. I had a blast coaching in it."

The only negative, I guess, is that we had to celebrate Thanksgiving in Hawaii. We were with each other and in paradise, which was cool, but most of the guys would've preferred the home cooking they were used to for Thanksgiving. They had a Thanksgiving buffet set up for us at a restaurant. We ate that and flew back to Kansas.

We opened Big 12 play that season at home against Kansas State on Jan. 4. The last time KU had lost a conference opener was 1990-91, when the Jayhawks lost their first two, at Oklahoma and at Oklahoma State — when they were in the Big 8.

It didn't happen this year, as we beat the Wildcats 67-49. That was Bruce Weber's introduction to the conference and the rivalry between KU and K-State. With his motion offense, the players were still learning his system and trying to do things they couldn't do. They weren't getting open looks. They shot 7-of-31 from the field. We shut them down. Not a lot was made of Coach Weber and how he took over for Coach Self at Illinois. We knew they weren't the best of friends, but not much was made of the whole "funeral" that Coach Weber had at Illinois for Coach Self.

> *"I can't remember specific moments from his career, but I remember during my senior year and his redshirt junior year how he was our best player for awhile, even in the first part of the conference schedule. Earlier in the conference, when we played at Oklahoma in our second conference game, he came up huge. We never really considered Oklahoma to be a tough team after my freshman year, but it was always tough to play in Norman. We knew we'd have to fight it out. In that game during my senior year, I was having a bad game, T-Rob wasn't playing great, and Elijah wasn't having a good game. Trav stepped up and hit a few (three) 3-pointers and a few and-one buckets (7-for-8 from the free throw line). He ended up led everyone in scoring (28 points). I remember that game specifically because if it hadn't been for him, we would've lost."*
>
> — *Tyshawn Taylor*

The other game I'll likely never forget was the Missouri game at Allen Fieldhouse on Feb. 25. Going into that game, we knew it'd be the last time we played them because they were bolting for the Southeastern Conference the next season. Adding to that, they had already beaten us that year in Columbia.

In the first game, we blew an eight-point lead in the last two minutes. We made dumb plays on the offensive end.

Marcus Denmon hit nine 3-pointers for Missouri. They had Kim English at the four spot, which was a hard matchup for us because he was coming off screens. But then Denmon hit three 3-pointers in the final 2:05, and they won, 74-71. That gave us some extra energy and a lot of excitement when we played them at the Fieldhouse.

They opened the game shooting lights out and jumped up early on us. Late in the first half, we realized we had to stop

Do not adjust your book — I'm not shooting this from my knees, but I am getting a shot over Missouri's Phil Pressey. As someone from Kansas City, Missouri, the rivalry games always had a little extra motivation. We beat Missouri 87-86 this game. It was the last time I faced them during my career — and the last time KU and MU played basketball against each other as members of the Big 12.

147

looking at the scoreboard and just start playing. We huddled on the court and someone shouted, "Stop looking at the scoreboard and just play!" We did. They were up by 12 at halftime, 44-32. Coaches came in there calm and cool. Coach Self didn't even go over the stats with us. He just told us, "Relax, come out and play our game. We can't make 12-point plays. We have to get some stops and make shots. And then know that in 20 minutes we're going to be in this locker room celebrating a win."

Early in the second half, we looked at the clock and told ourselves that they couldn't come in to our house and smack us like this. With less than 17 minutes left, they were up by 19 points, 58-39. We kept telling each other on the court that we had to keep chipping away. "Are we ready to play or what?"

We didn't tie the game until it was 75-75 with 16 seconds left, after T-Rob made a three-point play after being fouled by Michael Dixon.

Then, Missouri had the ball for the final shot. Phil Pressey tried to go in for a layup but T-Rob made an incredible block. That play was on my side. I was guarding Denmon, who was in the corner. Coaches said to stay with our man. Pressey went by my left side. I looked over my shoulder and saw T-Rob recovering and blocking the shot. The ball came right into my hands and I launched a shot. The ball left my hands but I don't think it would've counted. The place went nuts. I've never heard the Fieldhouse that loud. It was so loud that we couldn't hear Coach Self in the huddle. He couldn't draw anything for overtime; he just did hand signals, which was normal.

At the start of overtime, I got a rebound and threw it to Tyshawn who hit a 3. The whole game we felt the scoreboard was wrong. We knew we were in the game, and it suddenly felt that way with Ty's shot. Once we took that 78-75 lead, the weight was off our back.

In the final seconds, Denmon hit a shot that gave Missouri an 86-85 lead, but Ty, who was on fire the whole game, hit two free throws with eight seconds left. We held on for the 87-86 win.

A few weeks later, people started sending us video from both sides of the stands. We got a good laugh out of that when it was the Missouri side because of their reactions.

That's the second-largest comeback in Allen Fieldhouse history. Of course, it helps that we had that type of game against Missouri, and it was the last time we played them — at least in my time at KU.

The scoreboard told it all!

149

8 Senior Year: It's Been a Great Run

What's the old expression — time flies when you're having fun? Then that's the best reason to explain why my five years at Kansas flew by.

Going into the 2012-13 season, we felt good about the year ahead, but at the time we wondered who was going to step up to the plate for us. Looking across the board, Jeff Withey, Elijah Johnson and I were only role players. With Perry Ellis, Ben McLemore and the other newcomers we didn't know what to expect. Seeing the development of Ben during the previous year, we knew he'd have to be the guy to step up. He was a big scorer in high school and we needed him to do that for us. We didn't have another wing player who had been there long enough to know the system. Being there for a year without playing helped him a lot. It helps out a ton. It was an easier transition to the starting lineup for him than it would've been for Perry or anyone else.

Regardless of that unknown, I did know that it could be an unforgettable senior year.

Shortly before classes began that fall, we went to Europe to play four exhibition games in Fribourg, Switzerland and Paris. I don't believe more than one guy on the whole team had been to Paris, and I don't think any of us had been to Switzerland. It definitely was a trip we were looking forward to taking.

After winning our two games in Switzerland, we took a four-hour train ride to Paris. That was my first time on a train. It beat flying, that's for sure.

We did a lot of sightseeing. My favorite was the Eiffel Tower, which I didn't realize was lit at night. It was so cool because we happened to be down there at night, and once it got dark, the lights came on and started flashing. They talk about Paris being the "city of lights," and it's easy to see why.

That trip is memorable, also, because it's where my "Got 'Em" pictures on Twitter and Instagram started. On our first night in Paris I couldn't sleep because my body was still on Central Standard time. So a bunch of us were hanging out in the hotel lobby. As we walked by the elevators, we saw a guy lying down, sacked out. We walked by him a few times to see if he'd wake up. He was out cold. His hand was over his heart like he was doing the Pledge of Allegiance. We thought it was hilarious. We were recording video and making sounds to see if he'd wake up. Nothing. So, I ran behind him, made a funny face, giving a thumbs up, and we snapped a picture. I put it on Twitter with a "GotEm" tag. That was the first one. Fans loved it and wanted me to keep posting. So, the following day we were out seeing the town and I saw a guy in a lounge sleeping on the couch. I got him. (I didn't know what was up with Paris because people were sleeping all over the place.)

It happened again the next day. We were sightseeing at King Louis' castle and, of course, I spotted another victim. It was the middle of the day and he was lying out with his hands across his chest, holding a book. So, I got him. Whenever my teammates saw someone, they'd encourage me to take pictures.

I have pictures of my teammates but those aren't as funny, plus they're easy to get. I do have a good one of Coach Self, but I haven't posted it yet. I'll post it sometime soon.

By the time we left Paris, I had five "victims." And then fans, besides re-tweeting what I was posting, started taking their own

#gotem pictures and tagging me. People were tagging me five or six times a day. So I'd re-tweet those. That's how all of the "Got 'Em" pictures started. I have a blast with it. Now people think twice before taking a nap around me. The funny thing is that, more than a year later, it's still going.

Thankfully, our play on the court didn't continue through the year as we played in Paris. We were awful with plenty of things that needed work. We didn't think we'd start the season in the top 100 we were so bad. That experience humbled us and made

This is my first "Got Em" picture on Twitter and Instagram from Paris in 2012. A bunch of us were in the hotel lobby when we saw this guy, out cold. We thought it was hilarious and took a picture that I posted on Twitter and Instagram with the tag #gotem. More than a year later, fans are still taking similar pictures and tagging them. It's great!

us realize that we needed to get back to the States and learn to work as a team. Coach wasn't overly upset, since it was August and we were in Europe for exhibition games, but he wanted it to be a learning process for us.

Before our season officially started, we had Late Night at Allen Fieldhouse. I always looked forward to Late Night, but as seniors you want to make the most of the night. It's a chance to show the newcomers how we've improved during the summer. It's the first time for the rookies to see what it's like to run out of the tunnel for 16,000 fans. And then each class does a skit.

We performed "Gangnam Style" for our senior skit. At the time, the song was blowing up because everyone knew it. We tried to make it similar to what Psy did on the video. For our version, we wore black bow ties, white jackets and black pants. The crowd went nuts, and we had a blast.

When the season started — a few weeks later — it wasn't long before we had our first "real" test of the season. Coach Self likes to get a good mix of teams in our non-conference schedule, which helps us to prepare for the NCAA Tournament.

After opening with an easy win over Southeast Missouri State, we played Michigan State in the Champions Classic in Atlanta. We knew it'd be a tough game. Playing that game, we felt like we were going to win it from the jump. Even toward the end, we never felt we'd lose it. We had a lot of opportunities to win it but we didn't take advantage of them. They did and it showed on the scoreboard, 67-64. We had a bad taste in our mouths afterwards. But it was a good learning experience to show us that we weren't a great team. We knew we had to get back in the gym and work to get better.

Our first road test of the season came a little more than a month later, against another Big 10 team, when we went to Columbus, Ohio, to play our old friends the Buckeyes of Ohio State. At the time, they were No. 7 in the country; we were ranked ninth. We came in there with a lot of energy because we knew they wanted our heads as much as we wanted theirs. Since we beat them in the

Final Four the previous year, they were ready. We set the tone by hitting the first few baskets of the game. They came back at us. The whole first half was back and forth. With about six minutes left in the first half, the Buckeyes went up by eight, but we went on a run and took a two-point lead into the break.

In the second half we came out with even more energy to prove that we could win on the road. I was told later that, even though the game was on CBS, ESPN was doing cut-ins and talking about an "upset alert." In the second half, I started guarding Deshaun Thomas. We couldn't let him get going. It makes me feel good that Coach could call on me to guard the big scorers and playmakers. Coach talks about defense helping our chance to win. I always wanted to be the lockdown defender. It goes back to what my uncle said when we left his team and started playing AAU: Don't let your man score and have fun. It was never fun guarding someone like Thomas because it's a lot of work, but we held him to 16 points, and he made only 4-of-11 shots from the field. What made that day fun is that we won 74-66.

That was a good game before Christmas break. I'm using that term "Christmas break" loosely. Since it's near the halfway part of the season, there isn't much of a "break." Generally, we'd play a game around Dec. 22, have three days off, and then report on the 26th for two-a-days, and then our next game around the 29th. The only exception to that during my five years at Kansas was my freshman year when our games were on the Dec. 23 and 30.

Christmas break can make or break guys. If you aren't having a good season, the coaches are going to — let's just say — make the most use of your time when you come back. Some of the two-a-days were rough.

Thankfully, we had that good win at Ohio State to make post-Christmas practices a little easier.

After cruising past American for our post-Christmas break game on Dec. 29, we played host to Temple in a nationally-televised game on Jan. 6. Even though Temple was unranked and should've been a relatively easy opponent at home, we didn't play well in the first half. The 33-27 score was much closer than it should've been. I had a really rough first half. Even though I scored six points, I had one rebound, one assist, two turnovers and two fouls in 12 minutes.

Coach wasn't happy with me at halftime. And he let everyone know. That didn't happen often. I tried to make it hard on him to chew me out because of the way I worked. When he did chew me out, I couldn't help but start laughing because it was so uncommon. He'd be mad at first when I was laughing, but somehow it'd turn into a joke. This one during the Temple halftime was one of the biggest butt chewings he gave me in five years. He told me to straighten up and play harder. As I got into a habit of doing when Coach tried to get on me, I told him, "OK, don't worry, Coach; I got it. I'll change it."

> *"Against Temple, his man, Khalif Wyatt, was kicking our butt. I don't remember exactly what I said to Trav during halftime, but I'm sure I said something along the lines of: 'I thought you said you could guard! I thought you said you were the best perimeter defender in our league! This guy is just embarrassing us and you!' Probably something like that. Wyatt ended up with 26 points, but I do remember Travis had a big game."*
> — Bill Self

I came out in the second half and did my best to be a threat on both ends of the court.

I had to sit for about nine minutes during the second half because of foul trouble, but I ended the game with 14 points on a perfect day of shooting — 5-for-5 from the field, 2-for-2 from the 3-point line and 2-for-2 from the free throw line. The game led to my biggest shot in a KU uniform. With 35 seconds left and us leading 62-58, Elijah was trapped near the lane and he kicked the ball over to me on the wing. I hit a 3 that pretty much sealed the game. We won 69-62.

> *"It was fun to watch him around Coach Self, probably because they knew so much about each other. He went*

hard every day in practice and Coach never really got onto him. He'd give him a hard time when Travis was making shots and when he wasn't. He'd say something like, 'Trav, what are you doing? Why are you missing all these shots?' Trav would just say, 'Don't worry about it; don't worry about it. I got it.' And he did."
— Kevin Young, former Jayhawk

Our very next game opened Big 12 play in one of the craziest games of my senior year — and one of two wild ones against Iowa State during the season. The first was at Allen Fieldhouse.

We could tell then that it was going to be a wild Big 12 season, so the game itself shouldn't have surprised us at all. Coming into that game, we knew they were talented. They had guys who

During my senior year, I was in a bowling league. The other guys were (from left) Troy, Brad and C.T. It was a blast. I can't explain this but when I had a bowling game right after practice, I'd walk in and immediately get a strike. The guys told me I should always go straight from practice. There was a day when practice was running long and I had a bowling league game at 7. Coach Self said we had to hurry and wrap up practice. I chimed in, "Yeah, we gotta hurry so I can get to my bowling league." The guys gave me a hard time about being old and playing in a bowling league.

could shoot lights out. It was another back-and-forth game, but we were up at halftime, 42-38. Coach reminded us at halftime that we hadn't lost a conference opener in 21 years, and in order to avoid one against the Cyclones we'd have to step it up in the second half.

We did, but Iowa State wouldn't go away. They went up by six with less than 10 minutes left. With a few seconds left, Korie Lucious was at the line with a chance to put us away. We made sure we were telling him, while he was on the line, that his free throws could win it. He missed it and we got the rebound and called timeout. In the huddle, we thought they would foul us because it would've ended the game since they were ahead by three. As it turned out, their coach, Fred Hoiberg, told them not to foul. We ran the same play that the 2008 team used for Mario Chalmers' shot against Memphis in the championship game.

It's actually a standard play for us because it has so many options. The play is designed to take advantage of whoever is sleeping on defense. We would go over this play about 20 minutes in practice because of how detailed it is. We have to read the defense and be able to react quickly. Our first option against Iowa State was Ben McLemore, who had been on fire. I set the screen for Ben, he stepped behind me and took a shot that banked off the glass and went in, tying the game and sending it to overtime. At that point, we knew we had them. Their heads dropped. We blew the game open in overtime and won by eight, 97-89.

The funny thing is that it was a similar situation at their place a few weeks later. Lucious was at the line late in a back-and-forth game. I told him, "You better hit these free throws. This is the same thing that happened at our place." I was doing my best to get in his head. He told me he wasn't going to miss.

At the end of regulation, he had his head down and I poured a little salt in there. I said, "You should've won it when you had a chance."

The hot hand for us that game was Elijah. I never look up to see how many points our guys have because it doesn't matter. My man scored, though, so I looked up to see how many he had, which I'd do from time to time. I saw 33 next to a number 15. I couldn't believe it. I was trying to figure out who 15 was until it hit me that it was Elijah. He had an incredible game, ending with 39 points. Most of those (20) came in the final minute of regulation and overtime. He was a beast.

That was a wild game. About two minutes into the game, Coach was called for a technical, which was strange for him. (We later found out that he was trying to get T'd up to help fire us up.) Then, at the end of regulation, Elijah drove to the basket and the fans thought he charged. As the ball was loose, Iowa State's Georges Niang was called for a foul. The crowd went berserk.

Adding to the controversy, Elijah got the ball on a breakaway in the final few seconds with us up by 10 and went in for a dunk. Their fans and a lot of media types, as well as some KU fans, thought it was bad sportsmanship. If it were me, I would've done the same thing. It had been an emotional game in a hostile place to play. If they would've won the game, their fans would've literally run over us as if they'd won the national championship. They wouldn't have apologized, as Elijah did afterwards.

That was the 500th win in Coach Self's career. As Coach was walking off the court, an Iowa State fan charged him and was yelling at him. I'm guessing it was more over Elijah's dunk than it was to congratulate Coach on win No 500. Actually, I didn't see it happen and didn't know until we got back home that the fan charged Coach Self. A few days later we saw a T-shirt in Lawrence with the guy in handcuffs. It was pretty funny.

Sandwiched between the two Iowa State games, we played most of the Big 12 teams twice — at home and on the road. After winning our first four conference games, we headed to Manhattan to play K-State.

We knew Rodney McGruder was having a great season and making things happen for the Wildcats. Looking at film, the thought process was, if we eliminated him, who would step up? From what we could see on film, there was no one. If we cut the head off (their leader), no one would step up. Coach put me on McGruder.

The Wildcats run a motion offense that's easy to prepare for but hard to guard. If something happens on defense, they react. The key to that game was communication. We were telling each other where screens were coming from, and they were setting a lot to get him open. Most of the time, my back was to the play so I could keep an eye on McGruder. I got the credit for shutting him down because I guarded him, but it was a team effort. For that to work, all of our guys on the court had to work together and communicate.

Offensively, I took the shots the defense gave me and made open shots without forcing anything. I didn't realize this at the time, but I ended up leading our team that night in minutes played (36) and points (12). In all fairness, Ben and Jeff each had 11 points, and Jeff added 10 rebounds. McGruder ended with 13 points in 38 minutes. We won the game, 59-55.

"Travis was a willing defender from the get go. He bought into the defensive mentality that Coach Self preached day in and day out. Last year (2012-13), not being in the Kansas program, I got a chance to go to some games and watch some on TV. I was so impressed with the way he was scoring the ball. He worked extremely hard on his shooting. He started making the pull-up jump shot. Watching from afar, I was so happy for him. He was so deserving of all the accolades."

— Danny Manning

Overall, I feel that I did OK on both ends of the court. A lot of people don't understand how much energy it takes to chase around a guy like McGruder for 35-plus minutes on defense and then go down and play offense. You spend a lot of energy on defense in that type of game.

"K-State plays a motion offense, and of course, everything was centered around McGruder getting shots. On top of that, he may be the best-conditioned

athlete in our league. He's nonstop movement, and he got to the point where he really understood how to read screens and his teammates understood the right angles to get him open. Travis didn't shut him out, but instead of McGruder getting 15 good looks he probably got six. He could still score points when he was guarded well, but we limited his touches and Travis was the primary reason for that, obviously. He took pride in that. Deep down Trav thought he was a scorer, but I can guarantee that when he looked at the box score, the first thing he checked was how many points his man got."

— Bill Self

Three games later, after beating Oklahoma and West Virginia, we hit one of the most disappointing stretches of games in my five years at Kansas.

It all started on Feb. 2, at home against Oklahoma State. Their main player was freshman Marcus Smart. With all the hype around him, we knew he was a strong guard who rebounded. A key was going to be keeping him away from the glass and getting easy baskets. And that *was* the key. We didn't do what we needed to do against him and that's why we lost. We let him get comfortable. All 25 of his points were from the line or in the paint. I don't think he hit anything outside of the lane. I know he missed all five of his 3-point attempts. If we play that game over again and keep him from getting looks inside, we win. Even after giving Smart that many shots, we still had a chance to win. At their place, we had to fight for everything, but we handed them the game at our place, 85-80. We gave him confidence and they came in and beat us at home. It broke our winning streak, which was the longest in the nation at 18 games, and it ended our home streak, which was 33 games, second-longest in the nation. (Our last loss at home had been to Texas the day after Thomas Robinson's mom passed away.)

Four days later, Feb. 6, we went in Texas to play Texas Christian, a team that hadn't won a conference game.

Here I am posing with a fan after a game at Allen Fieldhouse during my senior year. One of the great traditions — at least in the last few years — has been signing autographs after our home games. The ushers rope off a section from the tunnel to our locker room. Fans line up on both sides, seemingly about seven or eight deep, and we walk down the line and sign autographs or have pictures taken. It's a mix of kids, KU students, and adults. For the most part, I didn't mind signing after games because people won't be asking for my autograph forever. KU fans will remember me, I hope, for years to come but I'll be able to walk down the street in any city other than Lawrence and not be recognized. The only aggravating part of the autograph line was when grown men would be there with bags full of stuff to get signed. It's obvious those guys are going to be selling the balls or jerseys or photos or whatever. I guess signing for the collectors (or sellers) is a necessary evil because we enjoy doing it for everyone else.

As the game started, it was obvious quickly that we weren't ready to play. TCU was making plays and we couldn't buy a basket. I missed something easy. Jeff missed a layup. Kevin missed a couple layups. We were over-thinking everything. One thing we kept thinking early — this can't be happening.

We were coming off a loss at home and going on the road to play the worst team in the conference. We didn't overlook them, because they had decent players. But we wanted to get in there, get the win and go home. Only problem was that we weren't ready to play. As seniors, we didn't step up and say anything or do anything to change what was happening. Everyone was on an island by themselves. I played 36 minutes and got only one point.

Coach said during his press conference after the game that we were the worst team Kansas ever had on the floor since Dr. James Naismith, the game's inventor, coached there. "I think he had some bad teams when he lost to Topeka YMCA and things like that in the first couple years," Coach said. "But for the first half, there hasn't been a team play worse than that offensively." We didn't know for a few days that he'd said that. We knew that things weren't good, so we all did our best to avoid the news. When we heard his comments, we weren't upset that he said that. We *were* an embarrassment. We scored 13 points in the first half against TCU. In 20 minutes, we made three baskets. Coach was pressured into apologizing to us, but I don't know why because he wasn't hurting our feelings. Fans, the media and others around school, I guess, took offense to Coach saying that, but they weren't out there getting beat by TCU.

After losing a home game and then losing to the worst team in the conference, we didn't know what to do. We didn't know what was happening. With a game at Oklahoma up next, we knew we had to execute or we'd lose three in a row. We couldn't let that happen. KU hadn't lost three games in a row since 2004-05. We started out playing OK but their guys stepped up and made plays. They beat us, 72-66. Of course, their fans stormed the court on us. When teams beat us at their place, they storm the court. That's another reason I didn't mind Elijah dunking at the end of the Iowa State game.

We then had about 48 hours to get ready for a rematch with Kansas State in Lawrence. Coach said, "The losing was last week. Let's forget about it and focus on K-State. We're not going to talk about those games anymore. Our fans aren't going to let us lose another game at home, so we're not going to let them down." We had a team meeting and tried to do all sorts of crazy things to figure out what was going on.

On Sunday, right before practice, we did the craziest thing that might've surprised some people — we did a "Harlem Shake" video. It was Justin Wesley's idea, which is why he's front and center in the video. Some guys didn't have a personality for it and thought it'd be corny. I didn't know what it was, but they showed me a few of the videos. I thought those were hilarious but we'd do the best one. I got the guys to do it who didn't want to do it because I was a senior. We all agreed to do it and just have fun. That's all we wanted to do was relax. We got everybody's costume and planned everything out.

We knew we had to get Coach Self involved. What's the worst thing he'd do, say no? I didn't tell him exactly what we were going to do, so immediately he told us no because he didn't want to dance. We told him that we didn't want him to dance anyway — believe me, we didn't want him to dance. We told him that we wanted him to write a play on the board, and then write "Harlem Shake," shake his head in disbelief and walk out. Surprisingly, he agreed as long as that was his role. We did two takes but we used the first one.

> *"Travis and Justin Wesley were the two who asked me to do it. I didn't even know what the Harlem Shake was. It turned out to be fun and it was cool to do. I was just a kid having some fun. The thing about it, and I know I'm biased, but even though we weren't the first ones to do a Harlem Shake video and teams like the Miami Heat did one after us, I really think that ours was about as good as any of them."*
>
> *— Bill Self*

That helped us take our minds off the games we'd lost. We thought everyone in Kansas was going to hate us for losing. Losing three in a row is not what Kansas does. The video was a way of getting back to us, which meant having fun.

ESPN showed the video the day of the game, which is how a lot of people saw it. We didn't know it'd be that big of a deal. We thought people would enjoy it but five million hits, at least as of the writing of this book? No way.

As it turned out, Jayhawk Nation didn't hate us. Coming out of the tunnel we could feel the energy of the crowd. After losing three games they were still screaming that way for us? I'm getting chills thinking about it now. Next thing you know, we were up by 20 points and went on to win 83-62. K-State coach Bruce Weber said they caught us at a bad time. I'd say so.

We were back to being Kansas.

That didn't mean easy games. After beating Texas by almost 30 points, 73-47, we played a revenge game at Oklahoma State. It had been 18 days since they beat us at the Fieldhouse. Stillwater is not an easy place to play, either. There was a lot on the line since they'd beaten us and that was Coach Self's alma mater. We watched film on that game and then they showed Marcus Smart doing the backflip on our court. It was a reminder of how that game went for us. We had to beat them at their place to win the Big 12 again, at least that's how we felt. We felt that way after every game following the K-State game.

We fought and fought against them, and the game went into double-overtime. It looked like we might be headed for a third OT, but with about 16 seconds left, Naadir Tharpe, who was playing for Elijah, who'd fouled out, hit a shot in the lane over Phil Forte that gave us a 68-67 lead. On the other end, I was guarding Markel Brown as he missed a shot. They lost the ball on the baseline and Forte, trying to knock it out of bounds off me, instead threw it off my leg and the ball went back in bounds. I turned around, dove after it and hit it opposite way before it went out of bounds. Ben grabbed it and went in for a dunk with no time on the clock.

Looking back at the stats, that was an incredible battle for us, with all of the seniors contributing, big time. I led the team with 18 points in 48 minutes. Jeff had another double-double with 17 points and 14 rebounds. Kevin had eight points, but 11 rebounds. And Elijah had 10 points.

We won our next three games, which included avenging the TCU loss (74-48) on Feb. 23, the Iowa State game in Ames, which I've mentioned, and then West Virginia at Allen Fieldhouse.

Next up was Senior Night against Texas Tech. I still get chills thinking about that night. Allen Fieldhouse will do that. I wasn't excited to leave, but I was looking forward to the night. It was a chance to experience the love from the fans one more time.

It was exciting to run out of that tunnel for the last time. I couldn't be sad because I got to experience that for five years, and had been coming to games since I was a freshman in high school. For guys like Jeff and Kevin, who hadn't been there as long, it might've been different. Elijah sat out the first two years of his career, basically, before becoming the main guy. For me it was another step closer to another goal and dream in life. It was a huge moment. My time was up. It was time to move on. I was more nervous about giving my senior speech after the game because I was freestyling.

The pregame video, as it always did, really got us going. Please don't take this the wrong way, but for what we'd been through a few weeks earlier, Texas Tech didn't have a chance. Coach told the younger guys before the game to go out and bust their butts because it was the seniors' last game at Allen Fieldhouse. We came out on fire and didn't look back. All 15 guys played as we won, 79-42.

Once again, each senior led by example on the court. Jeff led everyone with 22 points. Kevin had 14, I had 13, and Elijah had seven with 12 assists. And Ben, playing in what we all assumed was his last game at Allen Fieldhouse (and it was), had 13 points.

"Trav was the confidence of the team. As seniors, we all helped create the success we had during the season, but the biggest credit goes to Trav because he was there

longer than anybody else and it was his team. He was the most consistent player, and when things went really wrong he was there to lift everybody up. If someone did something wrong, Trav wasn't afraid to voice his opinion, but everyone knew he was saying something because he cared. He was one of our most consistent players because every night you knew what he was going to give us. He was the leader on and off of the court and I know he drove me more than probably anyone else did."

— Kevin Young

Then it was time for the speeches. Leading up to the night, Coach told us to write a few key points for the speech and to keep them short. I didn't write anything; I just freestyled to get it over with. Once you start talking it just kept going. I had the longest speech, I think, but I'd been there the longest so I had a lot to talk about. I gave a few personal shout-outs, but that's it. There wasn't a reason to thank everyone individually. It wasn't emotional for me or the other guys because the season wasn't over. We'd been through so much and were so excited for what was ahead; I think that's why no one cried during their speeches. We had another conference game and then we were planning on a good run in the NCAA Tournament.

"Everyone was asking if I was going to cry. I wasn't going to cry. It was emotional, but I wasn't going to show emotions. I was just so happy for Travis. Thinking about it, I'm going to miss all the people. I remember the first day and how the guys came out and helped him get his stuff out of the car. I think about him getting his degree in African-American studies. I think about how, while he was in school, I never heard anything bad about him, but I heard how he was so humble. I'll remember when he met Jennifer and had my grandson, TJ. Overall, I'm just glad he got to experience college. He turned out to be a good young man and a good dad."

— Venita Vann

Even thinking about it now, I'm not sad about not playing again in Allen Fieldhouse. The only thing now is that it won't be the same anywhere else I play. That might hit me in Belgium when I get in front of 3,000. I hear about the fans in Belgium and how they'll have 3,200 people and how it's a great environment. That's nice but it won't be Allen Fieldhouse. We had that many students camped out to get into the building. You miss that as a Kansas player. You don't get that in most NBA arenas, either. Guys like Paul Pierce, when they came back for the legends game, talked about how it'll never be the same.

Here's how crazy fans are in Allen Fieldhouse. I was known for wearing wristbands. Brandon Rush wore them in college, and I thought I'd keep the tradition going. Each senior had his own mark or tradition. Kevin had the fro. Elijah had the shoes. Jeff had the Withey sign, the "W" that fans made with their hands. We each had our niche with the fans. I didn't wear the wrist bands for the first few exhibition games of my senior year, and students asked me about it at school. So, I broke them out again. After every game at home, I'd throw them into the crowd. Fans were going nuts for these sweaty wristbands. People would go back and tweet about them. Fans who didn't get them would tweet about how they were close but they didn't get them, so they'll try harder the next time. Fans who got them, oftentimes tweeted pictures of the wristbands. It was crazy, but I got a kick out of it. There aren't many places in the country where that happens.

"Travis thought he had it all figured out all the time, and he usually did. I've said it before, but he wasn't good to coach, he was unbelievable to coach — he was terrific. He's one of my favorite players that I've coached because he tried so hard but he was so cool. If I was a college kid he'd be the first kid I'd want to hang with. He was a guy's guy. He certainly respected his position within our program and certainly was a good ambassador. He kind of reminded me of Aaron Miles — ornery but fun and certainly enjoyed life but

never compromised himself or our program in any way, shape, or form."

— *Bill Self*

I loved playing against North Carolina. This was from my senior year, when we played them at the Sprint Center in Kansas City in the NCAA Tournament. James McAdoo tried his best to block this shot, but I went in for two of my 22 points. This is a game I don't think I'll ever forget.

We ended the regular season at Baylor. Going into the day, we were in a tie with K-State for the Big 12 championship, our ninth straight. Unfortunately, they played earlier in the day and lost. All we had to do was beat Baylor and we'd be outright champs. When we saw they lost, we had that on our minds. Coach kept telling us to win the game so we'd win the championship outright. Baylor came out shooting lights out. Everything was going their way and nothing was changing that. They had the best nights of their lives and beat us, 81-58.

We'd won a share of our ninth-straight Big 12 title, but we weren't satisfied because we'd lost. The trophy was under the bus, which we didn't know until afterwards. Since we were used to winning the championship, Coach put the trophy in the middle of the locker room and congratulated us. (It's like the old expression of "act like you've been there before." We had, so we did.) A few days later we heard about K-State having a big party for theirs, which included cutting down the nets. We couldn't believe it! I guess that's how it is if you haven't won it in awhile and you have a fairly new coach.

"When I think back to Travis Releford, several things are going to come to mind. As a fellow Kansas Citian, I first heard about Travis when he was an eighth grader. He was on schools' radars then, which is a lot of pressure for a kid. You have to give Travis a lot of credit to get through all of that because not a lot of kids can handle that type of recognition. Then, when he got to KU, Travis became a glue guy, if you will. He was a great defender, but then he was solid in other aspects of his game. He reminded me a lot of one of my teammates at KU, Steve Woodberry. If you needed to lock somebody up, you had Woodberry do it, much like you'd have Releford do it. I think back to the first K-State game during his senior year, which kind of epitomized his entire career. He played more than 30 minutes (36) and chased Rodney McGruder

around hundreds of screens in that flex offense that K-State runs. I'll never forget that he looked over to Bill Self at one point, wanting to come out, and Bill wouldn't let him. Bill basically told Travis that he could sleep on the bus ride back to Lawrence. The other thing that has to be talked about with Travis is how he redshirted. I don't want to say that takes a lot of guts, but some guys look at that as if you're not good enough. But there's no better example of a redshirt year working than Travis' senior year. By his fifth year, he was great. If he doesn't take that redshirt in his sophomore year, obviously he's not there in 2012-13 and doesn't have the impact on that team that he had. As Bill continues to recruit huge classes because of guys leaving for the NBA early, there might be guys in Travis' situation — guys who have been in the program for a year or two and might be in a position to redshirt. They can look at Travis as an example of how they can work on their game, get bigger, quicker, and stronger physically, and contribute in a huge way to the team's success. I think Travis definitely left his mark on Kansas basketball in many ways."

— Greg Gurley, fellow Kansas Citian, former Jayhawk and color analyst on the KU radio broadcasts

We had a lot of motivation going into the Big 12 tournament because we knew if we won it, we'd get a high seed and probably play in Kansas City for our first two games of the NCAA Tournament. Besides, we wanted to prove we were the best team in the conference. We beat Texas Tech first. We wanted Oklahoma in the next round because they had beaten us. Instead we got Iowa State who we'd beaten twice and everyone said those were a fluke. That was motivation. We came in and played with a lot of energy, and beat them by 15. We knew we'd be playing

Baylor or K-State. The fans wanted to see K-State, but we wanted Baylor because they'd just beaten us. Instead we got K-State and we got the best of them, 70-54.

After that game, Coach Weber said something about how KU and K-State isn't much of a rivalry when they can't beat us. He's got a point.

What I didn't understand, though, is that he ended up winning the Big 12 Coach of the Year award. I don't think there's any way Coach Self shouldn't win the Coach of the Year until we lose the Big 12 regular season. We beat K-State three times during the season, but Coach Self doesn't get Coach of the Year? That doesn't make sense.

Regardless, another goal accomplished. Getting a No. 1 seed in the NCAA Tournament and staying in Kansas City helped give us a lot of confidence to go with the momentum. The tournament started with Western Kentucky. We knew they weren't a high-seeded team but they were going to be tough. They were well coached and had good players. Plus, we've witnessed how anyone can lose in the tournament. They came out with a lot more energy than we did, but we held on for the 64-57 win.

Next up was North Carolina. We loved playing big-name schools. Going into the game there was no pressure because it was North Carolina. Neither team was impressive in the first half, but they came out hotter than we did and took a 30-21 lead into halftime. Coach chewed us out again. We told each other, "Hey, this could be our last 20 minutes or we can make a run and continue our journey." As a Kansas City native, I didn't want my career to end there, in front of a lot of friends and family. So, I started attacking every chance I had. Ben wasn't having a good game and nobody was stepping up, so I figured I'd better. I knew how it felt to be treated as a Final Four player, so it gave me extra motivation. I wanted to eventually come back to Kansas for a national championship ring. I saw how those guys had a parade after 2008 and accepted their rings at Memorial Stadium. That was a goal. We'd already played in it so we wanted to win it. So I was all over the court.

I was mainly on Reggie Bullock. He ended with five points. We basically shut them down in the second half and pulled away for a 70-58 win.

The next weekend we'd be facing Michigan in Dallas in the Sweet 16. It was another fun game that we were looking forward to. They had a point guard, Trey Burke, who was one of the top guards in the country. We jumped out early on them. We were getting everything we wanted. I felt I was going to step up and make things happen for the team. Throughout the game I never imagined us losing. Never. We were up by 14 with a little less than seven minutes remaining in the game. Everything went our way until the last few minutes. We won the battle for the first 40 minutes and they won the most important five — overtime, which shouldn't have happened, if we'd done our jobs. We owned them. We just blew it. It happened so fast that I don't even remember how it started. We had five guys in double figures, led by Ben, who had a good game with 20 points. I had 16. It was drawn up

This was a game we felt was in our grasp, but Michigan made plays and took it away late. Much like the North Carolina game, I don't think I'll ever forget this one, but for a different reason. It ended up being the last time I'd play for the Jayhawks.

for us to make it to the Final Four but, just like that, it was over.

That's how it happens. Seeing Michigan playing in the national championship hurt. That could've been us. It comes down to match ups so I feel that if we'd gotten over that game, we could've beaten Louisville because of match ups. It's hard to swallow that we could've been playing for the title.

The season didn't end the way we wanted it to. But what a ride.

Jen and I were able to celebrate graduation with people who had a huge influence on my life (from right) Mike Gholston, his dad Mike Sr., and then Mike's fiancée Tamika.

9 These Jayhawks Will Always Be My Brothers

One incredible thing about playing at Kansas, whether it's for a year or, well, five, is the bond formed with teammates. Starting as freshmen, we go through summer camps and summer classes, to boot camp, to Late Night, to the season, to Senior Night, to (we hope) a long run in the NCAA Tournament. That's definitely the case with me. Even though I have five brothers and sisters — plus lots of cousins — the guys I played with for five years at Kansas are brothers to me. That'll never change.

The following are some random thoughts about each of my Jayhawk teammates — in alphabetical order — from 2008 through 2013.

Rio Adams:

Rio was a young guy, who didn't see eye to eye with Coach Self early. He didn't really understand how Coach Self coaches. After Paris in August 2012, I didn't think he'd come back with the way he and Coach got into it. But he completed boot camp and did everything expected of him. The way he played and the way Coach Self wanted him to play didn't match up. He showed he wasn't going change and felt it was best if he went to a different school.

Cole Aldrich:

Cole is a really goofy dude. That came across in how he played and showed off the court, in a good way, of course. The fans loved his goofiness, and he embraced it. He was smart at how he was portraying himself. He'd walk around without his tooth, for instance, and roll with it. he just didn't get it fixed, with his big head and tooth out, it was hilarious. Coach Danny Manning did a great job with Cole and the other bigs, helping them to improve their skill set as players. Cole didn't have a care in the world and he definitely didn't care what people thought about him, which is part of the reason everyone loved him.

Tyrone Appleton:

Tyrone was my roommate during my freshman year. We became close through that. He was like an older brother to me. He had been in college before, so he could help me out through the first couple weeks of conditioning and giving me brotherly advice. I only got to play with him for a year. As freshmen, our roommates were picked for us when we got to school. In the case of our class, since Tyshawn Taylor was from the same area as Quintrell Thomas, they were together. The twins were obviously together. Tyrone and me. Rio and Chase Buford. Once Quintrell and Tyrone transferred after that first year, Tyshawn and I became roommates.

Brennan Bechard:

Brennan and I played together only one year. He was a good guy to be around and he was a hard worker. Since he didn't play very often, the practices were his games and he knew that. He came ready to play. Coach would single him out and say how he was the toughest on the team and worked the hardest. Coach often used him as an example as someone who busted his butt to make the team better. Nobody outside of the team got to see that side of Brennan.

Chase Buford:

Chase put the team first. We all knew his dad R.C. was the general manager of the San Antonio Spurs, but Chase didn't flaunt that. He was down to earth. He was also incredibly basketball smart. He wasn't as skilled as some of the other guys, but he was out there competing and working his butt off every day.

Sherron Collins:

I was at Late Night when Sherron took his official visit. There were several guys. I was just there because I wanted to be at Late Night. I had seen him a few times at AAU tournaments, and he dominated games.

He played his first year, but not much. I thought he was one of the best guards on the team, so I had no idea why he wasn't playing. Coach wanted him to play a certain way. (Sound familiar?) He played a little more his sophomore year, and he really stepped up in the national championship game. He started KU's run but he doesn't get much credit for it because people only remember Mario Chalmers' shot.

Sherron had heart, which is what helped him. He was strong as a bull and extremely talented, but heart was the key to his game. He didn't let his height keep him from scoring or playing defense.

Perry Ellis:

Perry is very quiet. He's nice, but I don't remember having a full conversation with him because he's so quiet. He's very talented, of course. Kansas recruited him for awhile, so he's been around Kansas basketball since he was a lot younger. He's going to be a great player, which I think we'll start to see in 2013-14. He'll have to step up for the team, especially on the offensive end, but we saw late in his freshman year that he's capable of doing it once he learns the system better. He has range and good moves in the post. He really stepped up during the Big 12 Tournament.

Christian Garrett:

Christian is down to earth and very religious. He was the kind of guy who'd send out a mass text asking if there was anything he could pray about. Sometimes his family would have Bible studies at their place. We were roommates my last year, but he stayed with his mom a bunch. We made jokes about how his room was TJ's room because TJ slept in that bed more than Christian did that season.

C.J. Henry:

C.J. was a lot older than us. He was cool. He had already been a pro in baseball. We all felt he came to Kansas only to look after Xavier. Since he paid for school, it wasn't a huge deal. At some point he might've felt like he could've played. His dad Carl, who played at KU years ago, said in an article that C.J. could come in and take someone's spot, which didn't happen. Overall, C.J. and X were both cool. C.J. looked out for everybody. He just wanted a chance to play and be on the court with his brother. The age difference is so far apart that they probably didn't have that chance before.

Xavier Henry:

I didn't know much about X with the exception of the hype. He had a lot of family tradition at Kansas, so we knew he wasn't going to come in and sit on the bench. We had the same team coming back from my freshman year plus him. He was a good player, though. He was stronger than most of the kids his age. He was a kid in a man's body. He wanted to be a kid. If it was up to X, I think he would've stayed in school all four years just so he could hang out. Out of all the guys who went to the league, he came back to campus at every break. He didn't really want to leave, but with the way the NBA works, you have to go when it's hot. He enjoyed competing and being the top guy, but he wanted to have a normal life and just hang out with friends. He didn't want to be bothered with basketball for 24/7.

Elijah Johnson:

The first time I saw Elijah was on his visit. I didn't know who he was but he did a 360 under the legs dunk while wearing flip flops. It was the craziest thing I'd ever seen. I thought I was the best dunker on the team and I'd argue with anyone until I proved my point. When I saw Elij do that, I knew my time as the team's best dunker was limited.

He was very athletic. He was laid back and cool. He stayed to himself until we got to know him and then he opened up. Off the court he was quiet. He didn't get into too much stuff. My whole senior year he was my roommate on the road. We'd try to

No, this isn't for some magazine cover — just a few of us hanging out on campus. (From the top row) Elijah Johnson and Ben McLemore, me, Jamari Traylor and Naadir Tharpe. As the title of this chapter says, these guys along with a lot more from my time at KU, will always be my brothers.

help each other out to make each other look better as players. It played out well.

He hit a rough stretch of games in his senior year when he wasn't playing well. That stretch was tough for him because all fingers outside of our team were pointed at Elijah and Coach. Coach would say how the point guard was the quarterback of the team. He kept telling Elij that he was going to be the guy no matter what. "You're going to have to let last game go," Coach would say. "Just step your game up and not worry about stuff that's going on. To win, we're going to need you."

We were trying to help Elijah out because he went from the wing one year to handling the ball all the time. During our senior year, everybody had different roles. Elij had to step up as the point guard to know his role as well as everybody else's. It was new for him because he'd never played the point before. I always tried to encourage him. I told him we had his back. To win it all, he was going to have to get everything off his mind. He continued to work hard. He had to continue moving forward and just keep getting better. We saw a change in him. When he had his big game at Iowa State, everyone went crazy for him.

Elijah was a clown. He was into rapping. Throughout the season he'd make up raps. "Big Lij" was his nickname. After that Iowa State game, we were throwing water on him and we started his rap. The bad games didn't matter at that point. Coaches reminded him. He had a clean slate.

After the Iowa State game, the only negative thing he did was in the Michigan game. In the first few minutes, Elijah tapped Mitch McGary below the belt, we'll say. The refs didn't see it, they just saw McGary drop on the ground holding himself. They went to the monitor to see it.

During that time, we stood in front of the bench as Coach covered his mouth and gave Elijah a few words. This isn't necessarily a big secret anymore, but usually when Coach covers his mouth, he's cussing someone out. Sometimes he forgets to cover his mouth or doesn't care. He covered his mouth with

Elijah and went crazy. Because it was so early in the game, the level of foul that the refs could've given him would've gotten him kicked out. They didn't give him the flagrant and McGary missed both free throws, so it might seem OK. But Elijah got two quick fouls after that and played only 24 minutes. It was a dumb foul, and I'm sure Elij would admit that. That said, it wasn't that foul that cost us the game. We still could've and should've beat Michigan that night.

Like all "quarterbacks," Elijah was a big reason we were playing in the Sweet 16.

Jordan Juenemann:

Jordan was a great guy who was really into his faith. He went to Bible study every week. He encouraged guys. He was a hard worker on and off the court. He was another kid who, ever since he could pick up a ball, wanted to be a Jayhawk. He worked his butt off to say he played at Kansas. He and Tyshawn got into it all the time. When guys are on the red team, the practice squad, they don't have any cares. When you're on the red team, you can do whatever to keep your guy from touching the ball, but the blue team had to play completely within the rules. Jordan would do anything to keep Tyshawn from getting the ball or bringing it across halfcourt. It was funny to us, but Ty would get frustrated and mad. I think it helped Ty become a better player. Jordan helped everyone just so he could continue to wear a Kansas jersey. That's all he wanted to do.

Matt Kleinmann:

Matt was a guy who'd come in five minutes before practice and would get dressed and be out on the court before anyone else. One time, it got to the point where, before practice, guys would pick a time of when Matt would come in. Let's say practice started at 3:15. Guys were guessing 3:00 and even 3:13. He'd take off his street clothes, put on his uniform and ankle braces, with laces, in minutes. He was always the last one in the locker room but never the last one on the court. The whole team was in on it. Once he caught on to what we were doing, he had fun with it. I still don't know how he got ready so quickly. A great story about Matt is how, near the end of the 2008 national championship game, he took his warm-ups off so when he ran onto the court for the celebration it wouldn't be obvious that he had been on the bench. Christian did the same thing. I think that's pretty funny.

Merv Lindsay:

Merv was really young coming into college so we looked after him. He was big into music and getting music when it first came out. We called him "Music Man," because he made sure we were all hooked up with music when we went on the road.

Mario Little:

Mario came from a rough neighborhood growing up. He always talked about the "Chi," Chicago. When he was in school at KU, so much was happening in his old neighborhood. To see where he came from and how he's changed, he's come a long way. I don't know his back story completely but I'm sure it was similar to other guys. We've all seen and been through some of the similar things. "Rio" was another guy who did what it took for everybody to be OK. He'd go out of his way to help his teammates. I felt that's how every guy on the team was for all five years I was at Kansas. He was close with the twins.

Mario could score on anybody but me. I'd tell him that, too. He had moves. He was one of the best junior college players in the country, which says something. His time was off, though. If he'd come to Kansas a little earlier or a little later he might've had a different career. His cards didn't play out right. He was a better player than what fans saw. My last two years, he stayed in touch with me. He'd tell me to go out and do it for guys who didn't get that chance. When I'd play bad, he'd hit me up and see what was going on. We redshirted together, so we spent a lot of time together because we were always on the red team during practice and we sat on the bench together during games. He was a guy that when he left, he stayed in touch. He's a cool dude.

Landen Lucas:

Landen came in his freshman year and couldn't play because we had so many guys in his spot, so he redshirted. Since my situation was similar, he came to me for advice. I told him how that year was going to be his best year. When we win, you benefit from all of it, but it's all stress-free. In his case he has four years to perform. He was probably our best big man, scoring wise, this year. He could score at will. Withey couldn't score on Landen or stop him. Nobody got to see that. He has a chance to be a great player at Kansas. He'll be a problem for other teams.

Evan Manning:

Evan is a coach's son, so his basketball IQ is very high. He was out there competing every day and making guys better.

Ben McLemore:

Ben got screwed over, in Coach's terms, by the NCAA because he couldn't play at all in his first year at Kansas. That was good and bad. It paid off in the long run because he could still practice and learn different sets, and go through pregame. To experience all of that before you step in is huge. That relieved some of his pressure. He knew what to expect in his first year of eligibility. We knew it wasn't going to be a hard transition for him.

He's a very nice, quiet kid. It's odd but he's quiet with an outgoing personality. He doesn't say much on the court but he's got a fun personality. He's big into dancing. Obviously he's very talented. We saw that in his first year. The team got a lot better because of he and Jamari Traylor. When they were able to start practicing with us, the team really took off. It made the red team a lot better. They were using the practices as their games. No disrespect to the walk-ons, but Ben and Jamari added scoring threats to the red team. With walk-ons you know when you can take plays off. But with those guys, they were treating it as their game, which also made practices a lot more fun. I know what it's like; I made the most of my time on the red team early in my career.

Ben had serious bounce. One dunk that stands out was in Kansas City at the Sprint Center when he went over a kid and

While I was in Las Vegas getting ready for NBA tryout camps and then for the NBA summer league with Denver, I ran into a lot of former Jayhawks. Here I am one night with the twins, Markieff and Marcus Morris, Thomas Robinson, and Mario Little.

dunked it. His knee hit the guy and I think he went a little higher. On another, he was on the break at home and took off for a dunk. We were watching film in practice and Coach, who notices everything, said, "Did you see that? This kid took off from the free-throw line." He rewound it three or four times and kept calling Ben a "freak athlete." That was his term for guys who had serious bounce.

Brady Morningstar:

In high school, Brady had crazy bounce. It might've been me being younger and seeing him dunk, but I felt he could do a lot of dunks. He was cool. We liked the same type of music. He hung out with the guys I hung out with. Everybody on the team hung out together but when guys did certain things in smaller groups, like grab a quick bite to eat, Brady was out with my close friends in high school and in college. His dad Roger played at KU, of course. Both of them are hilarious. His dad always has a joke. In high school, his dad was my first AAU coach for Pump-N-Run. So I've known them for awhile.

Morris twins:

Even though Marcus and Markieff were two different people, they were one. So, it'd seem odd to break them up here. Marcus was more outgoing. He would start stuff. Little brother always into something. He was that way to Markieff. He didn't hold his tongue for anyone. He still was a nice guy; he was just more outgoing. Markieff was laid back and calm. He didn't let much bother him. They are two of the nicest guys ever. Everybody looked at them from the outside and saw them as tough, troubled kids from Philly. In the locker room, on the court and off the court, they were team and family first. Those two brought the whole idea of FOE (Family Over Everything) to the team. That's how they were. They had everyone's back, on and off the court.

Coach Self did a good job of keeping those guys together and fighting for each other. We were all brothers. Those are guys I can always call on. That's how they are. We hung out a bunch during this summer league when I was in Las Vegas after my senior year. They played for the championship. We all got to hang out and catch up with each other. Nothing's changed. We made jokes together. That's always going to be there. We're always going to be brothers.

Marcus and Markieff busted their butts after our freshman year. They were going to have to step up, and so much was being said about their games and how they couldn't do certain things. They wanted to prove everyone wrong and help the team. They started doing extra lifting, and going to the gym late at night to get extra shooting. We as teammates, noticed. You could see their improvement. They got bigger and then improved on the court. It paid off. They were both lottery picks.

I'm sure they're extremely happy that they're back together in the NBA. If you were ordering something for one, you might as well get it for two. I've never known twins, so to see those guys, it was wild. I remember one time Marcus and I had a camp in a small town in Kansas and Markieff had to stay in Lawrence. Marcus kept calling Markieff to check on him. They hadn't been apart that many days before in their lives — and it was only two or three days. It was cool to see but it was crazy. They did (and still do) everything together. All of their tattoos are exactly the same. The same one goes first every time. I think it's Marcus. I wish I had a twin after seeing some of that. They worked hard to get where they are today.

Tyrel Reed:

I sound like a broken record, but Tyrel is another guy who was really nice and a hard-working kid. I was surrounded by those guys on the Pump-n-Run AAU team. Tyrel was our point guard. They were all about team first, which is why we were so good at the time. Nobody was out there to jack up shots for themselves. On and off the court they were all about the team. It was Tyrel, Conner Teahan and me playing guards one year when I played up a grade level.

I'm sure we were a sight because Teahan wore a head band, Tyrel was the point guard, our big man was about 6-foot-7 and our four was a little taller than me. A team would come in and think they were going to blow us out. A white guy with a headband and shaggy hair. Tyrel on the point. Me as a skinny younger kid and then bigs who weren't big. We'd end up blowing teams out. Our teams were well coached. L.J. had us prepared to play. He prepared us for the future, not just our next tournament. We'd be doing actual workouts and there'd be dead periods when we'd do boot camp and then practice. Once I went to college, I was better ready. Other guys from AAU teams would say that they never practiced. We'd have 45 minutes of drills before we even touched the ball. When I got to college I was in incredible shape.

Niko Roberts:

Niko was another coach's son. He was a small guy and doing whatever he could to help the team win.

Thomas Robinson:

Thomas is a big-hearted, tough guy. He knew he had to work hard to step on the court. Coach let him know early that we didn't need him to score; we needed the best effort on the defensive end and get rebounds. He needed to use his motor and play hard all the time. He had a hard time figuring things out in his first year. The second year is when he went through everything. Working with Danny Manning, you could see that he was going to be the next great player at Kansas. He came a long way, though.

We knew he'd leave school a year early because he really had to for his sister. Coach was encouraging him to go. It would've been nice for him to come back, but that's just us being selfish. With all that was going on with him, the time was right. We told him that it's what God wanted him to do. I hope he can find his niche in Portland and get a lot of playing time.

Josh Selby:

Josh's time at Kansas flew. I remember him coming in, not knowing much about him. I saw videos of his crazy dunks. His very first day on campus he broke a finger. That set him out for awhile. Then he got into trouble with the NCAA, which was another setback. Then he hurt his foot, which was another setback. His timing was bad. I don't know everything he went through getting to Kansas, but I know he went through a lot at Kansas. His first game, which was at Allen Fieldhouse against USC on Dec. 18, 2010, he carried the team with 20 points, including the game-winning 3-pointer with 26 seconds left. With all the hype, we felt that was the guy we'd heard about. Three or four games later he was nowhere to be found. Coach was on him. It was a lot going on for him. He didn't get a chance. With all the hype going in, his chances were better at leaving. With he and Coach Self butting heads, I'm guessing he felt it was time to go. He was easy to get along with and he cared about the team but he kept to himself.

Tyler Self:

Tyler is the same as Evan Manning and Niko Roberts. As a coach's son, his basketball IQ is really high. It's like when Justin Wesley first came. You can see their improvement and confidence. Coach tried to pick on him a little but then he'd laugh about it.

Tyshawn Taylor:

Ty's my brother from another mother. My first day at KU I met him with all my shoes. He and Quintrell were out front. We've been tight ever since that first meeting. The second year we were roommates and became closer. He's very outgoing and outspoken, and a hard worker. We had similar backgrounds growing up. It was just Ty and his mom. She had boyfriends but his real father wasn't there for him. We'd go on about which place was tougher growing up: Hoboken, New Jersey or Kansas City. Our moms got along. He knew the things that would make me mad and I knew what would bother him. There's not a lot that would make me mad. He on the other hand, would start tripping on something and I'd have to say, "Let it go." He was playing quite a bit more than I was so he'd try to help me out at night. I just felt he was my brother the whole time I was in college. I called him "Little Bro" in public because I knew that bothered him.

Conner Teahan:

I've known Conner since high school. I'd see him playing at the Hy-Vee Shootout for Rockhurst, and then we played against each other twice when I was at Central. They beat us both times. Teahan and I played AAU together two years. He was a very, very nice guy. He's about his teammates. He put his teammates ahead of himself. He'd go out of his way to help anyone. He's been like that as long as I've known him. He was a great shooter, obviously. He had a bunch of shots that stand out. In high school he was playing against one of the Raytown schools at the William Jewell Tournament. He hit a three to send it into overtime and then he hit the game-winning three. He could shoot.

Naadir Tharpe:

Nad was another guy who worked hard and looked up to us for advice. We saw him as a little brother. Coach developed confidence in him. Early coach didn't have confidence in him, which threw Naadir off. He was worried about different parts of his game. Perry Ellis went through the same thing. It's tough to perform when you're learning the system and Coach expects a lot out of you as a freshman. It's tough to live up to the expectations, especially at a place like Kansas. Nad's been patient and worked hard. I think he'll definitely step up and lead the team in 2013-14.

Quintrell Thomas:

Quintrell was a very outspoken guy. He had a story about everything. If he didn't like something, did something or saw something, he had a story about. One story that stood out was about why he doesn't eat fish. He said he had a pet fish that was his best friend. He was gone to camp for a week and his mom forgot to feed it and it was dead. He told this long, drawn out story about why he doesn't eat fish. He had a different type of story every day. He was a nice person. He was cool. I missed him when he transferred.

As I mentioned earlier, recruiting is hit or miss. Not everyone pans out. Quintrell didn't. But we didn't pay attention to recruiting unless Coach told us to be on our best behavior because a guy who would help the team was going to be visiting.

Jamari Traylor:

Jamari reminded me of T-Rob, coming in with raw talent and a crazy motor. It seemed he never got tired and he worked hard. In the future, I know he'll be able to step up and help the team as much as T-Rob did with how well and how hard he played. Once you became teammates, you learn more about guys. To hear all that Jamari went through growing up, including being homeless, and how tough he was as a kid, it makes you think life hasn't been so rough after all. He's a tough kid. You could tell he knew he felt blessed to be in the situation he was in. He wasn't mad in his freshman year when he had to sit out. He was living the dream. I hope he can continue to get better and become a professional to help out his family. Hanging out, you'd never know he went through all he did before getting to Kansas. I hope he can help out his family through basketball.

Justin Wesley:

Justin's a comedian. As I mentioned earlier, he started the "Harlem Shake" video for us. If something was going on — a party or something at a frat house or whatever — Justin knew about it. In college, he was my PIC, my "partner in crime." When it came to going out, he was the guy for that. He made friends outside of basketball. It was good because you get the full college experience of knowing "regular" students from different states and backgrounds. I was that same way, which helped Justin and I click. We went out a bunch together, especially my senior year.

Andrew White III:

Andrew is a lights-out shooter. His first few days, I didn't know if he'd miss a shot. He's real quiet. He came into school stronger than everybody, but I don't know how. You'd think guys who lift a lot can't shoot, but he can. Once he gets his chance, he's going to really step up and be a fan favorite.

You don't want to mess with us playing paintball. The "us" in this case is me, Justin Wesley, and Jeff Withey.

Jeff Withey:

I've known Withey since before we got to Kansas because we were on the Adidas national team in Germany for a few weeks. He seemed like a cool guy, laid back. That hasn't changed. I never thought he'd end up at Kansas because he was headed for Arizona. A half-year later, he showed up in Lawrence. We talked about Frankfurt and that experience and how much fun we had. We've always been cool.

I didn't dream at all that he'd be the type of player he became. It was a combination of hard work and the coaches getting after him every single day. Early in his career he couldn't do anything right. Ask the coaches: he probably couldn't spell his name right. His first year (at Kansas), he either had to get better or he had to transfer. Coach would make him run all practice. All the time he'd make him do something crazy. Nobody thought Jeff would end up the way he ended up. It looked like he was a waste of talent and a waste of height. Coaches reminded him of that every day. He didn't work hard. His personality was so laid back and chill. He was like that on and off the court. Coaches didn't like that. They wanted him to get mad on the court, which wasn't him. They'd even get on him about the way he was stretching before practice. Coach is like that every year with at least one player. He's good at seeing potential, and if he sees it, he won't give guys a break. He'd remind guys that if he didn't care, he wouldn't be yelling. "If I'm yelling every day, that's to make you better," he's said once or twice or a hundred times. My freshman year, Tyshawn was the target. And then Jeff. My senior year it was Elijah and Perry.

Royce Woolridge:

Royce was a silly dude. He was a guy who didn't have a single care in the world. At all. We could be anywhere at any time and tell him to break out into a dance move, he'd do it right there, on the spot. He'd even do that in a grocery store. He loved dancing. I never knew someone who enjoyed it as much as he did. He

One of the reasons I went to KU was to get an education. Being the first from my immediate family to have a college degree is something special. Adding to graduation day was being able to see my teammates, such as Kevin Young, getting their degrees, too.

was younger than me, so I gave him advice because he was going through similar stuff that I went through. He was highly recruited. He committed to Kansas early. He probably thought he'd come in a play right way. He went a different route.

Kevin Young:

When Kevin first got to Kansas, nobody knew who he was. He just showed up. We had no idea who he was. Coach went on about how Coach Kurtis Townsend had seen him playing somewhere. He was one of the hardest working guys on the team and that continued when he got on the court. I don't remember a time, even in pickup games, when Kevin didn't play hard. In pickup games, you wanted him on your team because you didn't want to have to go that hard against him. Nobody could've imagined him playing for Kansas. He's only a little taller than me and I'm stronger than him. He's playing the four with guys who are bigger and stronger than me. His heart and his energy overcame his strength and skill set. He was one of those guys you want on your team. I talked to other guys in our conference and they talked about how he was all over the place.

There's not an easy scouting report on Kevin. Sometimes he got in our way. Coach hated it and loved it. He made plays for us when we needed it, but sometimes he got in our guys' way. Off the court he's a great guy. One of the first things he said to me, "Don't worry about passing me the ball because I'll just go get every rebound." He really meant that. He figured out a way to get his hands on the basketball. As far as the fro, we got used to it even though we'd tell him to get it shaped up or trimmed or something. Of course the fans loved it, so why change it?

I could make a lot of jokes about that group of teammates, but truth told, I couldn't have imagined playing with guys I enjoyed more than those Jayhawks. Indeed, they'll always be my brothers.

10 It's Not As Easy As It Looks

Two things could be said about my life up to this point: my dream — for as long as I can remember dreaming — has been to play basketball professionally. At least since middle school, when L.J. Goolsby put the thought into my head and helped me believe it was a possibility. The other thing that could be said about my life is that I don't give up. More to the point: I work tirelessly to prove my critics and the doubters wrong.

That said, there are two things to know as I write this chapter: I'm writing this from my apartment in Aalst, Belgium, as I work to prove the doubters wrong. More importantly, though, I'm a professional basketball player.

I'm currently playing for Okapi Aalstar. It's a great experience and an even better chance to work on my game and possibly be picked up by an NBA team.

The journey to get to this point was a fun, maddening, and an eye-opening whirlwind of a tour.

After my senior season at KU, I took a couple weeks off from playing basketball to unwind and get ready for whatever God had planned for the next step in my life. During that time, I started getting calls from agents, which is similar to the recruiting process in that you listen to how they can help your career. I thought I had a chance of getting drafted by an NBA team because agents were blowing my phone up. If they didn't think I had a chance, I don't think they would've wasted their time talking with me. After multiple conversations, I ended up going with Justin Zanik at ASM Sports. (In August 2013, Zanik became an assistant general manager with the Utah Jazz, so I went through a short interview process and chose J.R. Hensley at ASM.)

The pre-NBA Draft process is interesting. During the weeks leading up to the draft, you have a chance to show NBA teams what you can do.

Probably the biggest overall showcase is the Portsmouth Invitational Tournament, which was held in mid-April in Virginia. The PIT, as they call it, is a chance for seniors, who are on the fringe of being drafted, to play in a tournament in front of scouts and front office people from NBA teams. People hear about the NFL Combine. The PIT is about as close to the Combine as you'll find in the NBA.

While I was in Portsmouth, Justin was figuring out my pre-draft workout schedule for teams. For about a month before workouts began, I moved to Las Vegas to begin working out. I could've gone there or Santa Barbara, but I picked Vegas because I have an older brother, Deandre, who's lived out there for about six years. He's one of my biggest fans and harshest critics. He was a huge help throughout the process.

My first workout was with the Los Angeles Lakers. It was a week after they got eliminated from the playoffs. The important thing for that workout is that it gave me a feel for how the process would go. That's why Justin put me in that one.

And the process definitely was different than expected. I thought it'd be a couple of hours with a lot of craziness. It was very organized. You start out with a lot of testing and taking of measurements. That's followed by some drills on the court, and then a pick-up game in front of coaches and whoever else is making the decisions for the draft. As I went through the process, I learned that teams change up how they did the on-court workout, although they're all basically the same. With some, after the game, they have a one-on-one conversation with you, almost a full-blown interview.

IT'S NOT AS EASY AS IT LOOKS

After the workout with the Lakers, I went back to Vegas for a week before working out for Sacramento. With the Kings, the process was basically the same.

I did 10 workouts all together: the Lakers, the Kings, Indiana, Houston, Dallas, Atlanta, Orlando, Brooklyn, Detroit and Denver.

I was nervous with the Lakers because I didn't know what to expect. Once you go through the first one and then a couple others, you see they're all the same. Go in the night before, start the next morning. So, after that first one, I wasn't nervous at all. I knew what to expect. I was excited to go in, figure out who I was matching up against, and excited to get the workout in.

Justin heard feedback from a lot of teams that were interested in me, but they had to figure out other options and let Justin know. I'm sure most guys hear that throughout their process, but you don't know what's going to happen during the draft until your name is called.

Going into the draft, I felt like my chances were pretty good. Besides good workouts, I felt like I had a good senior season. It could've been better had we beaten Michigan and gone to the Final Four. Still, without that, Justin was saying it was a 50-50 chance that my name might get called. So I wasn't too disappointed after the draft. It was already set that I'd play on summer league teams, if I didn't get picked up. With that, there wasn't a lot of stress, because if you don't get drafted, you have to find a summer league team. I already had the option of Indiana and Denver, so the stress of scrambling to find a summer league team was gone.

I watched the draft with my family in Lawrence at my mom's place. We then headed out to Wayne & Larry's, a restaurant in Lawrence, to catch the second round. Watching the draft, knowing that you have a 50-50 chance of getting selected, you view it differently. You pay attention to what types of players teams are drafting. If a team picked a wing player in the first round, for instance, you know they aren't likely going to take another wing in the second round. Of course, my name wasn't called, which was OK. There wasn't a need to get mad about it.

With that out of the way, I worked out with the Pacers for a few

Freddy Van Geit for Okapi Aalstar

Here I am driving in for a basket in an early season game. Our coach, Brad Dean, writes a blog on the team's website, www.okapiaalstar. be. I'm humbled that his first post of the season was dedicated to me joining the team. I'm even more blown away by a couple of the things he wrote. "With Okapi he will find himself much more in focus on offense. Shooting over 60% from 2's and bombing away at plus 40% says a lot about his offensive capabilities. Throw into the mix that his reputation was built as a defensive stopper we feel we have found ourselves a well-rounded player. We cannot forget he is a rookie and a transition period will be needed. A priority for the sportive cell has always been to bring in quality people. It is difficult to find a negative word about Travis - the person. Hard-working and unselfish on the court and respectful and honest off... that is the kind of people we want playing for and representing Okapi. Releford should fit in nicely."

days in early July at their practice facility in Indianapolis. I played with a lot of veteran guys who had been in the league and had been out of school for several years. There were only two first year guys, me and Christian Watford, who was a four-man at Indiana. I knew him throughout the Adidas Nation camps. We met at the airport and went to the workout together. Immediately, we noticed that a lot of the guys had been out of school for a few years, including Micah Downs, who played at KU briefly. You expect a bunch of first-year-out guys, but it was guys who'd go overseas and come back to try to make a team. (The process never stops until you quit trying or keep playing overseas.)

It was interesting to talk with Micah, because I never knew why he left KU. He said the time wasn't right. He had stuff going on back home and he wasn't getting along with Coach Self, so he felt like he had to leave. Looking back, he said, he regretted it. At the time, though, he had to do what he had to do. As I mentioned earlier in the book, throughout my time at KU, I saw guys come and go, so I know it's part of the process. The KU basketball circle of life, if you will. Micah ended up being cool. He asked me how I liked KU and if I liked Coach Self. (Of course, my answer to both is a huge YES!) He gave me advice about the whole professional process.

After Indianapolis, I went to Denver to work out for the Nuggets and then play on their summer league team. So I worked out in Denver with a few of the guys from their staff before going back to Vegas, which is where they played in the summer league. That was the one time that it was more like an individual workout, at least in Denver. Once we got to Vegas, we started having team practices and putting in a few sets for summer league. That was it. Then we started playing.

The guys playing for the Nuggets were a mix, just like with the Pacers, except there were more veterans. That's one thing I didn't understand about the summer league. I thought it'd be guys fresh out of school, but the majority of the guys who play in the summer are veterans, who are still trying to make the league or even guys who are signed already. We had a bunch of second- and third-year guys who were already signed, which made it tough for us first-year players. It felt like first-year guys didn't really get a chance to show what we had because we're going to be on the bench more than the guys already signed, of course.

The great thing about playing in the summer league in Vegas was that it was almost a Jayhawk family reunion. The Morris twins were playing for Phoenix (and they ended up playing for the championship). T-Rob was playing for the Blazers. And then Elijah, Jeff and Ben were all out there with different teams. We were able to watch each others' games because there were only two gyms. I'd try to check out their games. We met up a few times to go see other guys. So, I met up with Mario Little, who was out there, along with T-Rob and a few others to watch the twins. I saw Ben play in a game. We played against Jeff's team once. So, it was cool to see my former teammates and see how they felt about the whole process. At the time, Elijah, Jeff, and I were the only ones unsigned. Jeff signed with New Orleans shortly after the summer league.

> *"There's a place (in the NBA) for kids like Travis, he just has to get with a program that values the things that he does. He's an underrated defender, he's improved skill-wise dramatically over the last years, and he's started to shoot the ball better. One thing that happens in the NBA, unfortunately, a lot of times they focus on what you can't do instead of what you can do. That's not everybody but if you can play and they recognize the things that you do, you'll have a chance. Everybody is looking for a lockdown defender, and I think Travis does that extremely well, and he is really a team first guy which I think most people still value."*
> — *Larry Brown, Hall of Fame coach*

My plan-B, if things didn't work out with an NBA team, was to play in Belgium. I had already signed a contract, which allowed me to continue to try to make a team in the States. If I got picked up, the contract would become void. Since I didn't, I came over here.

Like many of the other parts of this professional journey so far, I was both excited and nervous about coming to Belgium. Besides the unknown, there's the whole idea of being in a foreign country, away from family and friends, for 10 months. And, as big as that for me was not knowing whether I'd like the food, whether I'd like my coaches and teammates, and whether I'd like my living arrangements. Luckily, that didn't all hit me at once.

All I could do was hope for the best. As I write this, it has been the best. The best of the best has been the arrival of Jennifer and T.J. They got here a few weeks after I did, and they'll stay as long as I'm here. On top of that, it's exciting to get back to playing again as part of a team. My teammates and coaching staff are cool. Most of the guys on the team are older and have been pros for several years, and they're fun to hang out with. The adjustment is a lot easier when you have good teammates. The fan base is crazy — nothing like Kansas — but they're sold out for most games, from what I've been told. At least they have a waiting list for tickets. Coming from the best

Freddy Van Geit for Okapi Aalstar

This is my new "home court" in Belgium. It's not quite Allen Fieldhouse — it seats less than a third of the Fieldhouse — but we have great fans, although it might not appear that way from this picture. This was taken during one of our early exhibition games.

fan base in the United States to rabid fans here, is huge. Fan support always gives you another reason to compete. A lot of places throughout Europe aren't like this.

On the court, the competition seems good, so far. The play is more physical with more pushing and grabbing. The referees in the States try to clean up the game. The biggest rule adjustment here is that, if I'm on a fast break and the ball is thrown to me, I have to catch and drop it before taking a step. You have to get used to that. In the U.S. you can get two or three steps on a fast break and go in for the basket without dribbling. That's how I've done it my whole career. Here, I just have to remember to put it on the ground immediately. But the guys are good enough to be paid players. The players just aren't quite as good as they are in the NBA or as hyped as the NBA.

> *"I thought Trav had a shot to be drafted but I think he's better off in the position he's in now because he can pick and choose his future and where he ends up. The way it played out is that he could go where he wants to go, tryout for what team he wants to try out for. It's probably not going to work out early on in his career but this is fitting for Travis. He's going to have to earn his way back and do some things. Yeah, I wish he would've been drafted and I wish he was on an NBA roster. I talked to several teams about him and what he can become. I do think he'll play in the league at some point in time but he's going to have to go and tighten some things up in his game. The more you watch him, though, the more he grows on you. So if he was just given an opportunity I think he can make his way, but he's going to have to prove himself and put up some numbers before he gets a serious shot. Again that's the story of his career. That motivates him and drives him. He's not soft; he's tough and if he wants something he will go after it. And he definitely wants this."*
>
> *— Bill Self*

IT'S NOT AS EASY AS IT LOOKS

♦ ♦ ♦

Aalst, Belgium, is a city with a population of roughly 87,000. I've enjoyed the town. I'd guess that 90 percent of the people here speak English, which helps. The other main languages spoken are French and Dutch. One of my teammates can speak all of them. All of the guys speak English, but a few of them can speak two or three languages. When we're together, we all speak English. Sometimes the coaches and a couple players might talk in another language, but for only a bit. That helps with the culture shock. Some guys go to places overseas to play and nobody speaks English except a translator. That'd be tough. I'd even say that about 80 percent of our television channels are English-speaking channels. The only channel I don't have is ESPN, but I'm keeping tabs on the internet.

Freddy Van Geit for Okapi Aalstar

At the end of September, our team won the Belgian Supercup by beating Oostende, 73-60. Da'Sean Butler, who played at West Virginia and is standing behind me in this photo, led all scorers with 21 points. I had 11. The cool thing is that we had a huge crowd at the game. After this picture was taken, our coach, Brad Dean, took the trophy over to our fan section and let them pass it around. How crazy is that! Could you imagine us winning a tournament at Kansas — say the CBE Classic at the Sprint Center — and then Coach Self taking the trophy to our fan section to pass it around?

Another of my main concerns was the food. I actually like it. I've always been big on pasta, so I eat a bunch of spaghetti. Their fries are great. The Belgian waffles are incredible!

These people are crazy about their beer. Unfortunately (or fortunately), I don't like the taste of beer, so I can't really comment on whether it's good. After our fist preseason game, they fed us at the gym and then walked around serving us cups of beer. I passed them on to my teammates. We had just finished playing and we were playing the next day and they were passing beer around? Oh, but they love their beer.

◆◆◆

We haven't gotten too far into our season yet, and obviously I have no idea what the future holds. Whenever I've decided my playing career is finished and I've taken it as far as I can, I'd like to become a college coach. I learned so much during my career from Coach Self and all of the assistants at Kansas that I feel I could pass along some of that to other guys who want to take this game as far as they can.

> *"I think Travis would be great at telling kids how to play angles. I think he could be an effective recruiter because he reads people well and people like him. He's not a flamboyant guy. In fact, he's probably the least flamboyant guy on the team but everybody wants to hang with him. He's the coolest kid on the team, without question. It doesn't matter what group he's with, everybody knows that. I think he could be a very effective coach when he quits playing."*
>
> *— Bill Self*

> *"His credibility would help him as a college recruiter and coach. He could say, 'I have been in your shoes. I've had to redshirt to continue to work.' He understands it's a process and a journey to evolving. He hasn't come close to reaching his potential. What he accomplished, where he came from as a young man and a player is unbelievable. He went into it with an*

open mind an open heart. He wanted to get better. In this day and age, there aren't a lot of kids who open up like that and still remain a confident player and young man. I think he'll be successful in whatever he does. He wanted to be a part of the program at Kansas that he came in and worked hard every day. That took everybody around him to another level. If you're going against him, you know you have to have your motor turned up. Same if you're playing with him. The motivation that he brought to that intensity level was really good. He had a unique trait of being a great teammate, even when he's talking trash on the court. The guys respect that. They enjoyed the challenge but he wanted them to do well. It's easy to cheer for guys who play well, but especially for guys who want others to play well. That's Travis."

— Danny Manning

In the meantime, though, I'm going to keep working hard at improving as a player and staying on this ride, whether that

Not a bad view in Brussels when we went to dinner at the Hard Rock Café.

means playing in Europe for a few years, or tweaking some parts of my game and making it in the NBA.

> *"I think there are a million Travis Relefords in this league — guys who are great teammates, come in and work hard every day, good defenders who can play different positions. Maybe they aren't Hall of Fame guys or All-Star players, but they're contributing to their teams. I think it's a matter of time for Trav. I may be biased, but I'm a huge Travis Releford fan. Every team needs a Travis Releford — a guy who's going to come in, dive for loose balls, lockdown the opponent's best defender, and make some shots. If you ask him, he's always been a great shooter, but just like me, he had to work on his shot in college. He put in a lot of extra work to where he's not just a dunker and a slasher, but he can shoot it, too. I think Coach Self said this first: Travis isn't a great shooter, but he's a guy who makes shots. Every team has a player like Travis Releford. It's not an ideal situation to go overseas first, but at the end of the day, this is about bettering yourself and helping your family. Obviously he wants to get to the league, and I think this is just a step in the right direction for him. I'm happy that he came this far based on all he went through at KU, especially with the redshirt. He handled everything unlike anyone I've seen. I'm definitely rooting for him."*
>
> *— Tyshawn Taylor*

This is about proving what I can do and doing something I love, but also helping people who are instrumental in my life.

When my mom was struggling to put food on the table, because of what I was seen as a top player in the Kansas City area, people would want to step up and help. People would see my family struggling and try to help. Sometimes it was family members and sometimes friends of family members.

This is a way to help our family. Where I'm from, you want to do what you can to help the family. This is a path to help give my mom and family motivation and hope. I don't want them to stress about certain things in life as they have for years.

Really, this is my first real job and first real chance to help my family, financially. Sure, I cut some grass and shoveled snow off driveways, but I never had a job where I went and filled out an application.

Of course, when I was at Kansas, my dad, the comedian, would joke: "You better practice filling out an application if you keep playing the way you're playing." He was just messing with me, thinking he was funny, but I'd say the same thing to him that I'd sometimes say to Coach Self, "Yeah, yeah; I got this."

And that holds true today. "I got this."

Through everything that I'm doing and everything that I've done, I hope I'm a great example to T.J. I hope he learns that I'm a hard worker who fights through adversity, and I've never given up when times have been hard.

Of course, having a child has affected my decision-making because his present and his future go into everything I do.

Jen, TJ and me at a carnival in Aalst, Belgium, in October 2013. And, yes, I'm a Jayhawk, whether I'm in the States or Belgium. Always. Rock Chalk!

Looking at my career now and wherever God may lead me, I have to think about him and make sure he's alright. That's what my family did for me — and I think I've turned out alright.

As most anyone who's had a child can attest, when you have a kid, your mindset changes. You focus more on the child. Since at least middle school, I've wanted to play professional basketball. However, I'm pursing this dream not only for me, but also for TJ.

24 Slam Dunks With #24:

1. *Favorite breakfast spot in Lawrence:* First Watch

2. *Favorite lunch spot in Lawrence:* 23rd Street Brewery

3. *Favorite dinner spot in Lawrence:* Indian Palace

4. *Favorite night spot in Lawrence:* The Hawk

5. *Best barbecue in Kansas City:* Too hard to pick just one because we have so many good ones.

6. *Favorite hang out in Kansas City:* At home with my family or at the gym.

7. *Favorite movie of all time:* Almost any movie that stars Will Ferrell.

8. *Favorite TV show of all time:* "Walking Dead"

9. *Favorite actor:* Will Ferrell

10. *Celebrity crush:* Megan Fox

11. *Favorite "person" to follow on Twitter:* WTF Facts

12. *One item I can't live without:* My phone

13. *Thing I'll miss most about KU:* Everything

14. *Biggest fear:* Flying

15. *Sporting event you'd most like to attend:* Soccer game in Europe because it's so big there.

16. *Pregame superstitions:* Never wear my earrings to the game. I feel like I would play bad if I did.

17. *The guy I enjoyed guarding most:* I didn't enjoy guarding anyone because the person I always had to guard could shoot at anytime, so there were never any breaks on defense for me.

18. *Biggest shot I hit for KU:* The one against Temple at Allen Fieldhouse.

19. *My best dunk while at KU:* Windmill dunk against UMKC.

20. *Most memorable dunk by another Jayhawk:* When I threw it off the glass to EJ (Elijah Johnson).

21. *The guy on the floor (besides me) who talked the most smack (KU or opponent):* The twins.

22. *Funniest KU teammate:* EJ or Mario Little

23. *My message to young athletes:* Don't ever let anyone tell you that you can't do something. Or, if there are a lot of people saying it, use it as motivation to prove them wrong. Through all of your ups and downs, keep your confidence.

24. *The one person in history (living or dead) I'd like to meet:* James Naismith, so I can thank him for creating the game of basketball.

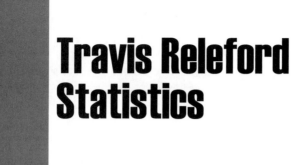

Travis Releford Statistics

Releford 2008-09 Game-by-Game (Freshman)

OPPONENT	MP	FG-A	PCT	3PT-A	PCT	FT-A	PCT	O-D-T	PF	A	TO	BS	ST	TP
UMKC	13	3-3	1.000	0-0	---	0-0	---	1-1-2	2	1	0	0	2	6
FGCU	15	4-8	.500	0-1	.000	0-3	.000	2-0-2	1	0	2	0	0	8
$vs. Washington	3	1-2	.500	0-0	---	2-2	1.000	0-0-0	1	0	0	0	0	4
$#vs. Syracuse	1	0-0	---	0-0	---	0-0	---	0-0-0	0	0	0	0	0	0
Coppin State	13	3-6	.500	0-0	---	2-5	.400	3-0-3	2	0	2	0	0	8
Kent State	3	2-2	1.000	1-1	1.000	0-0	---	0-1-1	1	0	0	0	0	5
New Mexico State	5	1-3	.333	0-0	---	0-0	---	2-1-3	0	0	1	0	0	2
Jackson State	6	1-1	1.000	0-0	---	0-0	---	1-1-2	0	0	0	0	0	2
$Massachusetts	4	0-0	---	0-0	---	0-0	---	0-0-0	0	0	0	0	0	0
Temple	6	0-1	.000	0-0	---	0-0	---	1-0-1	2	0	0	0	0	0
at Arizona	8	1-3	.333	0-0	---	0-0	---	2-0-2	3	0	0	0	0	2
Albany	14	3-4	.750	1-1	1.000	0-0	---	0-4-4	0	2	1	0	0	7
Tennessee	8	0-2	.000	0-0	---	1-2	.500	1-3-4	0	0	0	0	0	1
Siena	8	2-2	1.000	1-1	1.000	0-0	---	1-1-2	3	1	1	0	1	5
at Michigan State	21	0-2	.000	0-1	.000	0-2	.000	0-1-1	2	0	0	0	0	0
*Kansas State	3	0-1	.000	0-0	---	0-0	---	0-0-0	1	0	1	0	1	0
*at Colorado	5	0-0	---	0-0	---	0-0	---	0-0-0	3	0	2	0	0	0
*Texas A&M	9	0-2	.000	0-1	.000	1-2	.500	1-1-2	0	0	0	0	2	1
*at Iowa State	1	0-0	---	0-0	---	0-0	---	0-0-0	0	0	0	0	0	0
*at Nebraska	6	2-2	1.000	0-0	-	1-2	.500	0-3-3	1	0	0	0	0	5
*Colorado	2	0-0	---	0-0	---	0-0	---	0-1-1	0	0	1	0	0	0
*Oklahoma State	7	2-4	.500	0-1	.000	1-2	.500	0-0-0	0	0	1	0	0	5
*at Missouri	8	3-4	.750	0-0	---	3-3	1.000	1-1-2	1	0	1	0	0	9
*at Kansas State	5	1-1	1.000	0-0	---	2-4	.500	0-0-0	0	0	2	0	0	4
*Iowa State	5	0-0	-	0-0	---	0-0	---	0-2-2	1	0	1	0	0	0
*Nebraska	11	1-2	.500	0-1	.000	1-1	1.000	1-0-1	1	0	1	0	0	3
*at Oklahoma	10	0-0	---	0-0	---	1-2	.500	2-0-2	3	1	1	0	0	1
*Missouri	5	0-0	---	0-0	---	0-0	---	0-0-0	0	1	0	0	0	0
*Texas Tech	9	2-2	1.000	0-0	---	0-0	---	1-3-4	0	0	2	0	1	4
*Texas	10	1-1	1.000	0-0	---	2-2	1.000	0-1-1	1	0	0	0	1	4
@$ vs. Baylor	0	0-0	---	0-0	---	0-0	---	0-0-0	0	0	1	0	0	0
vs. Dayton	1	0-0	---	0-0	---	0-0	---	0-0-0	0	0	1	0	0	0

^ indicates starter, * = Big 12 Game, $ = played in Kansas City, # = Overtime, @ = Big 12 Championship, NCAA Tournament

211

Releford 2010-11 Game-by-Game (Sophomore)

OPPONENT	MP	FG-A	PCT	3PT-A	PCT	FT-A	PCT	O-D-T	PF	A	TO	BS	ST	TP
^Longwood	19	3-4	.750	0-1	.000	1-2	.500	1-1-2	1	2	1	0	0	7
^Valparaiso	15	2-2	1.000	1-1	1.000	0-0	---	1-0-1	3	0	2	1	1	5
North Texas	18	1-4	.250	1-3	.333	1-2	.500	0-1-1	2	1	2	0	0	4
TAMU-CC	20	5-6	.833	1-2	.500	0-0	---	0-1-1	0	2	0	1	0	11
vs. Ohio	16	5-8	.625	3-6	.500	0-0	---	2-1-3	0	2	1	0	0	13
vs. Arizona	18	4-6	.667	2-3	.667	0-1	.000	2-2-4	1	1	1	0	2	10
UCLA	9	0-1	.000	0-1	.000	0-0	---	1-1-2	0	1	0	0	0	0
vs. Memphis	9	2-3	.667	0-0	---	2-2	1.000	2-0-2	0	0	2	0	0	6
$vs. Colorado State	11	2-4	.500	0-1	.000	0-0	---	2-3-5	1	0	1	1	2	4
^USC	15	0-2	.000	0-1	.000	1-2	.500	1-0-1	1	0	0	0	2	1
^at Califronia	18	1-2	.500	0-0	---	2-3	.667	2-0-2	3	0	0	0	2	4
Texas-Arlington	16	3-5	.600	2-3	.667	0-0	---	1-1-2	1	0	1	0	1	8
Miami (Ohio)	12	0-3	.000	0-1	.000	0-0	---	0-3-3	0	5	0	0	1	0
UMKC	18	4-7	.571	2-3	.667	3-4	.750	1-1-2	2	0	1	1	1	13
at Michigan	4	0-0	---	0-0	---	0-0	---	0-0-0	0	0	0	0	0	0
*Kansas State	1	0-0	---	0-0	---	0-0	---	0-0-0	0	1	0	0	0	0
*at Texas Tech	9	0-3	.000	0-3	.000	0-0	---	0-0-0	1	2	0	0	0	0
*at Nebraska	2	0-1	.000	0-1	.000	0-0	---	0-1-1	0	0	0	0	0	0
*Missouri	16	4-5	.800	2-2	1.000	0-0	---	0-3-3	2	1	0	0	1	10
*Iowa State	13	0-2	.000	0-2	.000	2-3	.667	0-1-1	2	1	1	0	0	2
*at Kansas State	10	1-4	.250	0-1	.000	3-4	.750	2-0-2	1	0	0	0	0	5
*@Colorado	5	1-1	1.000	0-0	---	0-0	---	1-0-1	0	0	1	0	0	2
*Oklahoma State	14	1-2	.500	0-1	.000	1-2	.500	0-1-1	1	1	0	0	0	3
*at Oklahoma	4	0-0	---	0-0	---	0-0	---	0-0-0	0	0	0	0	0	0
*at Missouri	1	0-0	---	0-0	---	0-0	---	0-0-0	0	0	0	0	0	0
@Colorado	1	0-0	---	0-0	---	0-0	---	0-0-0	0	0	0	0	0	0
vs. Boston	5	0-3	.000	0-1	.000	0-0	---	1-0-1	0	0	1	0	0	0
vs. Illinois	1	0-0	---	0-0	---	0-0	---	0-0-0	0	0	0	0	0	0
vs. Richmond	2	0-0	---	0-0	---	0-0	---	0-0-0	0	0	0	0	0	0
vs VCU	1	0-0	---	0-0	---	0-0	---	0-0-0	0	0	0	0	0	0

^ indicates starter, * = Big 12 Game, $ = played in Kansas City, # = Overtime, @ = Big 12 Championship, NCAA Tournament

Releford 2011-12 Game-by-Game (Junior)

OPPONENT	MP	FG-A	PCT	3PT-A	PCT	FT-A	PCT	O-D-T	PF	A	TO	BS	ST	TP
^Towson	25	5-7	.714	2-4	.500	2-2	1.000	0-1-1	3	3	2	0	2	14
^vs. Kentucky	28	2-6	.333	0-2	.000	0-0	---	0-3-3	0	0	5	0	2	4
^vs. Georgetown	29	4-4	1.000	0-0	---	2-2	1.000	2-2-4	3	0	3	1	1	10
^vs. UCLA	33	3-8	.375	2-3	.667	0-0	---	1-1-2	1	2	0	0	2	8
^vs. Duke	33	2-6	.333	0-2	.000	0-0	---	3-2-5	1	1	1	0	1	4
^Florida Atlantic	33	5-9	.556	0-2	.000	1-3	.333	0-6-6	3	4	1	2	1	11
^South Florida	28	2-3	.667	1-2	.500	0-0	---	0-3-3	1	3	2	0	1	5
^Long Beach St.	29	4-9	.444	0-3	.000	2-3	.667	0-1-1	4	2	4	0	1	10
^Ohio State	32	3-5	.600	1-2	.500	3-4	.750	1-4-5	2	2	1	0	2	10
^$Davidson	35	2-3	.667	0-0	.000	4-7	.571	1-5-6	3	0	0	0	4	8
^at USC	28	0-2	.000	0-1	.000	3-4	.750	1-1-2	0	2	1	0	0	3
^Howard	20	1-1	1.000	1-1	1.000	3-4	.750	1-3-4	0	1	1	0	0	6
^North Dakota	31	5-10	.500	1-4	.250	3-8	.375	5-2-7	2	1	0	0	1	14
^*Kansas State	30	6-11	.545	2-4	.500	2-2	1.000	6-5-11	2	1	3	1	0	16
^*at Oklahoma	34	9-13	.692	3-5	.600	7-8	.875	2-1-3	3	2	0	0	2	28
^*at Texas Tech	32	3-8	.375	2-4	.500	4-6	.667	1-1-2	1	1	0	0	3	12
^*Iowa State	36	3-9	.333	1-3	.333	0-0	---	4-3-7	3	3	0	0	1	7
^*Baylor	36	5-7	.714	0-1	.000	1-2	.500	1-2-3	2	4	2	0	2	11
^*at Texas11	34	2-7	.286	0-2	.000	0-2	.000	1-5-6	3	1	0	1	0	4
^*Texas A&M	33	4-8	.500	0-3	.000	0-0	---	0-5-5	4	4	0	0	1	8
^*at Iowa State	40	3-5	.600	2-3	.667	2-3	.667	0-2-2	3	4	0	1	0	10
^*Oklahoma	33	9-13	.833	1-2	.500	1-2	.500	3-3-6	0	1	1	0	0	12
^*at Missouri	29	2-7	.286	1-2	.500	0-0	---	1-2-3	4	3	1	0	1	5
^*at Baylor	24	5-7	.000	0-0	---	1-2	.500	2-1-3	2	3	2	0	1	1
^*Oklahoma State	33	5-6	.833	0-0	---	0-0	---	2-2-4	2	2	1	0	0	10
^*at Kansas State	29	2-7	.286	0-2	.000	0-0	---	1-5-6	1	0	0	0	1	4
^*Texas Tech	27	3-4	.750	2-2	1.000	4-4	1.000	2-3-5	1	3	0	0	2	12
^*at Texas A&M	28	2-6	.333	0-2	.000	0-1	.000	2-5-7	4	2	0	1	1	4
^*Missori	34	1-7	.143	0-3	.000	5-8	.625	2-1-3	0	2	1	0	2	7
^*at Oklahoma St.	32	1-2	.500	0-0	---	2-4	.500	0-2-2	3	1	0	0	0	4
*Texas	27	2-5	.400	0-1	.000	1-2	.500	3-2-5	2	2	0	0	1	5
^@vs. Texas A&M	32	2-2	1.000	0-0	---	3-4	.750	1-1-2	3	2	1	0	1	7
^@vs. Baylor	31	3-5	.600	0-1	.000	0-0	.000	4-3-7	3	2	1	0	0	6
^vs. Detroit	29	1-5	.200	1-5	.200	2-2	1.000	0-3-3	3	1	1	0	1	5
^vs. Purdue	24	4-7	.571	0-2	.000	2-4	.500	4-2-6	4	0	0	0	1	10
^vs. NC State	31	3-9	.333	0-2	.000	1-1	1.000	2-2-4	0	2	1	0	2	7
^vs. North Carolina	36	4-6	.667	1-2	.500	2-4	.500	1-2-3	1	0	1	0	2	11
^vs. Ohio State	38	5-7	.714	1-1	1.000	4-4	1.000	2-4-6	1	1	0	0	2	15
^vs. Kentucky	30	1-6	.167	1-2	.500	1-2	.500	0-1-1	5	1	0	0	1	4

^ indicates starter, * = Big 12 Game, $ = played in Kansas City, # = Overtime, @ = Big 12 Championship, NCAA Tournament

Releford 2011-12 Game-by-Game (Senior)

OPPONENT	MP	FG-A	PCT	3PT-A	PCT	FT-A	PCT	O-D-T	PF	A	TO	BLK	ST	TP
^&SE Missouri State	34	3-11	.273	0-5	.000	3-3	1.000	2-3-5	2	2	4	1	1	9
^!Michigan State	36	2-6	.333	0-1	.000	4-4	1.000	0-2-2	3	3	2	1	4	8
^&Chattanooga	33	1-6	.167	0-5	.000	0-1	.000	1-3-4	3	6	3	1	2	2
^&Washington State	23	6-7	.857	2-3	.667	3-3	1.000	0-1-1	3	1	0	0	0	17
^&Saint Louis	36	7-13	.538	4-7	.571	5-6	.833	0-1-1	2	0	1	0	1	23
^San Jose State	37	5-6	.833	1-2	.500	2-2	1.000	1-3-4	0	4	1	3	0	13
^Oregon State	38	8-10	.800	0-0	.000	4-4	1.000	3-4-7	3	5	2	0	2	20
^Colorado	28	5-8	.625	0-2	.000	0-0	---	1-1-2	2	6	0	0	1	10
^Belmont	29	6-9	.667	2-2	1.000	3-3	1.000	2-3-5	0	4	2	0	3	17
^Richmond	29	4-5	.800	1-1	1.000	2-2	1.000	1-1-1	1	2	1	0	2	11
^at Ohio State	38	4-5	.800	1-2	.500	2-4	.500	0-4-4	1	1	3	0	0	11
^American	23	7-8	.875	5-6	.833	0-0	---	1-1-2	0	3	0	0	0	19
^Temple	23	5-5	1.000	2-2	1.000	2-2	1.000	0-4-4	5	1	2	0	0	14
^*Iowa State	39	3-6	.500	0-2	.000	6-8	.750	2-2-4	3	2	1	0	0	12
^*at Texas Tech	33	4-5	.800	0-0	---	4-4	1.000	0-3-3	0	1	0	0	3	12
^*Baylor	35	2-6	.333	0-3	.000	6-6	1.000	1-4-5	2	2	3	1	2	10
^*at Texas	35	4-8	.500	0-2	.000	4-4	1.000	1-3-4	2	2	2	1	2	12
^*at Kansas State	36	5-6	.833	2-3	.667	0-0	---	0-1-1	0	3	0	0	1	12
^*Oklahoma	38	4-10	.400	1-4	.250	1-2	.500	0-5-5	1	5	3	1	1	10
^*at West Virginia	28	7-9	.778	1-1	1.000	0-1	.000	0-4-4	2	2	3	0	2	15
^*Oklahoma State	38	2-5	.400	2-2	1.000	2-2	1.000	2-1-3	4	3	0	0	3	8
^*at TCU	36	0-1	.000	0-0	---	1-2	.500	3-3-6	5	4	1	0	0	1
^*at Oklahoma	35	3-7	.429	1-2	.500	1-4	.250	1-8-9	1	1	2	0	0	8
^*Kansas State	22	4-8	.500	1-3	.333	1-1	1.000	3-1-4	4	2	1	0	0	10
^*Texas	31	5-7	.714	4-5	.800	1-2	.500	1-4-5	2	3	0	0	0	15
^*at Oklahoma St.	48	7-10	.700	0-2	.000	4-7	.571	2-4-6	1	1	3	0	1	18
^*TCU	30	4-5	.800	1-2	.500	3-3	1.000	0-2-2	3	1	2	0	1	12
^*at Iowa State	42	6-12	.500	5-9	.556	2-4	.500	1-3-4	2	3	3	0	2	19
^*West Virginia	25	2-8	.250	0-3	.000	2-2	1.000	0-0-0	2	2	2	0	1	6
^*Texas Tech	28	2-3	.667	1-1	1.000	8-10	.800	2-3-5	0	2	0	0	1	13
^*at Baylor	36	1-6	.167	0-2	.000	0-0	---	3-0-3	4	2	2	0	1	2
^#Texas Tech	31	2-4	.500	0-1	.000	2-2	1.000	1-1-2	1	5	3	0	2	6
^#Iowa State	36	3-9	.333	1-6	.167	2-2	1.000	4-2-6	1	2	2	0	0	9
^#Kansas State	36	3-7	.429	0-1	.000	0-0	---	0-3-3	3	2	1	0	3	6
^$Western Kentucky	37	4-6	.667	0-1	.000	3-5	.600	2-1-3	2	1	1	0	1	11
^$North Carolina	38	9-13	.692	1-1	1.000	3-5	.600	3-5-8	2	0	2	0	3	22
^$Michigan	42	6-10	.600	0-0	---	4-4	1.000	0-5-5	1	6	1	0	1	16

^ indicates starter, * = Big 12 Game, & = CBE Classic, ! = Champions Classic, # = Big 12 Championship, $ = NCAA Tournament

2012-13 Season/Career Highs

Points
Season 23 vs. Saint Louis (11-20-12)
Career 28 at Oklahoma (1-7-12)

Rebounds
Season 9 at Oklahoma (2-9-13)
Career 11 vs. Kansas State (1-4-12)

Field Goals
Season 9 vs. North Carolina (3-24-13)
Career 9, twice
last vs. North Carolina (3-24-13)

Field Goal Attempts
Season 13, twice
last vs. North Carolina (3-24-13)
Career 13, three times
last vs. North Carolina (3-24-13)

Three-Point Field Goals
Season 5, twice
last at Iowa State (2-25-13)
Career Same

Three-Point Attempts
Season 9 at Iowa State (2-25-13)
Career Same

Free Throws
Season 8 vs. Texas Tech (3-4-13)
Career Same

Free Throw Attempts
Season 10 vs. Texas Tech (3-4-13)
Career Same

Assists
Season 6, three times
last vs. Michigan (3-29-13)
Career Same

Steals
Season 4 vs. Michigan State (11-13-12)
Career 4, twice
last vs. Michigan State (11-13-12)

Blocked Shots
Season 3 vs. San Jose State (11-26-12)
Career Same

Minutes Played
Season 48 at Oklahoma State (2-20-13)
Career Same

Miscellaneous	Season	Career
10+ Points	26	48
20+ Points	3	4
5+ Rebounds	13	31
2+ Assists	27	54
2+ Steals	14	33
2+ Blocks	1	2
Double-Doubles	-	1
Led KU in points	8	10
Led KU in rebounds	2	2
Led KU in assists	8	10
Led KU in steals	13	25
Led KU in blocks	-	2

Travis Releford Career Statistics

Year	GP	GS	Min	Avg	FG	FGA	Pct	3FG	FGA	Pct	FT	FTA	Pct	Off	Def	Tot	Avg	PF	FO	Ast	TO	Blk	Stl	Pts	Avg
2008-09	32	0	225	7.0	33	58	.569	3	8	.375	17	32	.531	20	25	45	1.4	29	0	6	22	0	8	86	2.7
2010-11	30	4	303	10.1	39	78	.500	14	37	.378	16	25	.640	20	21	41	1.4	22	0	20	15	4	13	108	3.6
2011-12	39	38	1206	30.9	119	239	.498	26	80	.325	68	104	.654	62	102	164	4.2	83	1	69	37	7	46	332	8.5
2012-13	37	37	1252	33.8	155	270	.574	39	94	.415	90	114	.789	43	99	142	3.8	73	2	95	59	9	47	439	11.9
TOTAL	138	79	2986	21.6	346	645	.536	82	219	.374	191	275	.695	145	247	392	2.8	207	3	190	133	20	114	965	7.0

Travis Releford Career Big 12 Conference Statistics

Year	GP	GS	Min	Avg	FG	FGA	Pct	3FG	FGA	Pct	FT	FTA	Pct	Off	Def	Tot	Avg	PF	FO	Ast	TO	Blk	Stl	Pts	Avg
2009	15	0	96	6.4	12	19	.632	0	3	.000	12	18	.667	6	12	18	1.2	12	0	2	13	0	5	36	2.4
2011	10	0	75	7.5	7	18	.389	2	10	.200	6	9	.667	3	6	9	1.0	7	0	6	2	0	1	22	2.2
2012	18	17	571	31.7	58	119	.487	14	39	.359	30	46	.652	33	50	83	4.6	40	0	39	11	4	18	160	8.9
2013	18	18	625	34.7	65	122	.533	19	46	.413	46	62	.742	22	51	73	4.1	38	1	41	28	3	21	195	10.8
TOTAL	61	34	1367	22.4	142	278	.511	35	98	.357	94	135	.696	64	119	183	3.0	97	1	88	54	7	45	413	6.8

Travis Releford Career Postseason Statistics

Year	GP	GS	Min	Avg	FG	FGA	Pct	3FG	FGA	Pct	FT	FTA	Pct	Off	Def	Tot	Avg	PF	FO	Ast	TO	Blk	Stl	Pts	Avg
Big 12	7	7	167	23.9	13	27	.481	1	9	.111	7	8	.875	10	10	20	2.9	11	0	13	11	0	6	34	4.9
NCAA	13	9	314	24.2	37	68	.544	5	17	.294	22	31	.710	15	25	40	3.1	19	1	12	9	0	14	101	7.8

Releford's Honors & Accomplishments

- Danny Manning "Mr. Jayhawk" Award (2013)
- All-Big 12 Second Team (2013)
- Big 12 All-Defensive Team (2013)
- Athletic Director's and Big 12 Commissioner's Honor Rolls (Fall 2012, Spring 2013)
- Big 12 Player of the Week (Nov. 26, 2012)
- CBE Hall of Fame Classic MVP (2012)
- Big 12 Player of the Week (Jan. 9, 2012)
- Finalist for 2011 Dunk of the Year (Windmill dunk against UMKC — Jan. 5, 2011)
- Las Vegas Invitational All-Tournament Team (2010)
- Athletic Director's and Big 12 Commissioner's Honor Rolls (Spring 2009)
- Eastern Kansas League Player of the Year (Bishop Miege, 2006-07 and 2007-08)
- DiRenna Award finalist (2008)
- Member of USA Basketball Men's U18 National Team (2008)

- Member of the USA Basketball Men's Youth Development Festival White Team (2007)
- Gatorade Kansas Player of the Year (2008)

About the Authors

Freddy Van Geit for Okapi Aalstar

Travis Releford went to the University of Kansas as a highly touted basketball recruit out of the Kansas City area. After being the odd man out during his freshman season, Releford accepted a redshirt during his second year. For the next three seasons, Releford became the player that everyone anticipated him being: a gritty defensive specialist who could carry the Jayhawks when needed. He became so valuable by the end of his senior year that coach Bill Self called Releford the "rock" of the Jayhawks. Following his senior year, during which he was once named Big 12 Player of the Week, Releford was a second team All-Big 12 performer and selected as a member of the Big 12's All-Defensive Team. Releford is currently pursuing a professional playing career in Belgium.

Matthew Hicks/MSH Photography

Matt Fulks, a Kansas native, is the author/co-author of nearly 20 books, including "For Jayhawks Fans Only" and "A Good Place to Stop" (with Max Falkenstien). After somehow being allowed to graduate from Lipscomb University in Nashville, Tenn., Fulks pursued a journalism career that has allowed him to work in nearly every form of the media. He lives in the Kansas City area with his wife Libby, their three kids, his mid-life crisis Jeep, and a Weimaraner named after Elvis. Sort of.

Visit www.ascendbooks.com for more great
titles on your favorite teams and athletes.